Reinventing the Wheel

Linda Sloan

GAZELLE
P R E S S

Reinventing the Wheel
by Linda Sloan
Copyright ©2008 Linda Sloan

ISBN 978-1-58169-303-4
For Worldwide Distribution
Printed in the U.S.A.

Gazelle Press
P.O. Box 191540 • Mobile, AL 36619
800-367-8203

TABLE OF CONTENTS

Acknowledgments

I want to begin this book by giving all of the glory to Jesus Christ, my Lord and Savior. Praise you Jesus for your revelation and understanding brought forth for these end times.

I have been extremely blessed by the mentors God has given me. In particular, Eava Currence has truly lifted me up upon her shoulders to launch me into my anointing and God-given purpose. She has not only been a spiritual mother to me but also led me down a path, which allowed me to receive the revelation for this piece. In many aspects Eava's teaching is the foundation of this book, whether it came through specific words given or seeds planted. Thank you Eava, you have no idea how much you've blessed my life.

My husband, Eric, has inspired me tremendously. His apostolic gifting has helped me to solidify so many prophetic visions and put them into understandable translation.

Finally, I want to give special thanks to my editor, Karen Fornof. She has inspired and encouraged me beyond expectation. She had a very difficult job, and I believe a special place awaits her in heaven for her perseverance and steadfastness.

Foreword

We are witnessing a global shift in how the world does business—a new economy of outsourcing and offshoring. Without a shift in our mindset, our existing economy will falter and eventually fail.

Reinventing the Wheel opens our eyes and minds to a revolutionary business structure that helps business leaders not to just survive, but to thrive in the new economy. This new way of business is inspired by the ancient book of Ezekiel. It can be summed up with two contrasting pictures: a triangle and a circle.

The triangle represents the traditional business structure—a rigid pyramid shape that focuses on command and control. Take a look at the typical organization chart. Within this hierarchy, all eyes are on the leader and on serving the leader's vision. The implied imperative from leadership is "Your job is to serve me." Also, as the triangle goes upward, there's less and less room for advancement.

The circle represents a revolutionary business structure that encourages creation and collaboration. The leader in this structure is at the hub of the wheel. But the focus is not inward on the leader. The focus is outward—along the spokes of the wheel—to the employees of the organization and outward to the customers. The foundational thought is "Your job is to serve others."

The leader's job in this scenario is to equip and empower the employees. The goal, however, is more than just to do a job—it's to fulfill a calling. As employees grow and become passionate about their calling, the organization grows. As employees advance, they are trained to create new hubs in which they serve those around them. Unlike the triangle structure, the circle is dynamic, fluid, and flexible.

The triangle is about self-exaltation and power trips. The circle is about empowering others to grow.

Our example is Jesus. He served those He led. He trained His disciples, equipped them, and empowered them. Then He sent them out to do likewise. In three years, they advanced from disciples to apostles. Jesus charged them in turn to disciple nations. Jesus' business model turned the world upside down.

This book may just do the same, because biblical examples aren't just for churches and synagogues. When we apply the ancient wisdom of the Bible to business structure, revolution happens. The circle could very well be the new revolution.

John Fornof
Impact Creative Media, Inc.

Introduction

The title of this book is unique in that it uses a common idiom, *Reinventing the Wheel*, along with a word that is rarely used, *transfiguration*.

Reinventing means "to make over completely; to bring back into existence or use; or to recast something familiar or old into a different form."[1] This book is literally about reinventing the purpose of the wheel and applying it to the structure of business. The first six chapters address the root of what has blocked many individuals and businesses, both physically and spiritually, from reaching their full potential. There are reasons why the glory of God, which brings signs, wonders, and miracles, has not been fully manifested in the marketplace. Very specifically, it is rooted in the mindset and physical structure of the pyramid, which is the fundamental structure of organizational charts throughout the world. In it, the leader sits on top of the pyramid as a king sits on a throne.

Chapter seven introduces a revelatory structure based on the wheels as seen by the prophet Ezekiel. It is about a heart change as well as a physical structural change. The second part of this book is about walking out of the curse and into the blessing. This is a process of transfiguration.

The word *transfiguration* is a rather obscure word that is rarely used. Most Christians would recognize it from the Bible but do not use it in their daily conversation. Transfiguration means "a marked change in form or appearance: a metamorphosis; a change that glorifies or exalts."[2] The purpose of this book is to bring a metamorphosis to the marketplace that ultimately exalts and brings glory to God. If you are willing to allow this transfiguration into your life and place of business, God's glory will manifest.

This book is a prophetic revelation submitted to the end time believers called to bring God's kingdom into the marketplace. Ask the Holy Spirit for the apostolic anointing to receive what this prophetic word means to you and how to apply it to your business or assignment in this season.

I pray the following over each one of you:

Lord, bring wisdom, revelation, healing and deliverance to each person reading this book. Bring each one through Your process of transfiguration to the place where he or she will begin to see miracle after miracle. Establish in each individual the dominion that You gave to man and woman in the garden to win more souls to Christ than ever before. Bring forth truth that will equip them to influence not only people's lives on earth, but also their souls and legacy for all eternity. In Jesus' name, amen.

CHAPTER 1

Miracles Began
in the Marketplace

Several years ago while I was in prayer, God spoke to me, "Linda, I am bringing the 'fivefold ministry' into business." This came as quite a surprise to me given that I didn't even know what the fivefold ministry was. I diligently asked for insight from my pastor, but all he shared was, "It is referred to in Ephesians. Look it up!"

And He Himself gave some to be apostles, some prophets, some evangelists, and some pastors and teachers, for the equipping of the saints for the work of ministry, for the edifying of the body of Christ, till we all come to the unity of the faith and of the knowledge of the Son of God, to a perfect man, to the measure of the stature of the fullness of Christ (Ephesians 4:11-13).

I could grasp this Scripture for the church, but I struggled with how these five offices could function in the workplace. Then as I read the gospels and the book of Acts, it became very clear to me that God used common people to do miraculous things! Jesus and many of His disciples were laymen, and they transformed the world.

Jesus was a carpenter (see Mark 6:1-4). Peter, Andrew, James, and John were all fishermen (see Matthew 4:18-22). Matthew was a tax collector, the local IRS Agent (see Matthew 9:9). Jesus continued to add disciples to His group until He had twelve. They were called disciples while in their training process of learning and following Him. He then released power into them and called them apostles or "leaders with authority." It is important to acknowledge that once they understood the authority that they walked in, Jesus could release them into their anointing.

> *And when He had called His twelve **disciples** to Him, He gave them power over unclean spirits, to cast them out, and to heal all kinds of sickness and all kinds of disease. Now the names of the twelve **apostles** are these: first, Simon, who is called Peter, and Andrew his brother; James the son of Zebedee, and John his brother, Philip and Bartholomew; Thomas and Matthew the tax collector; James the son of Alphaeus, and Lebbaeus, whose surname was Thaddaeus; Simon the Canaanite, and Judas Iscariot, who also betrayed Him* (Matthew 10:1-3, emphasis added).

Many who are called into the marketplace walk in an apostolic anointing. They are leaders with God's given authority, but few understand what that is and how to operate in it. "The Greek word translated *apostle* in English means quite simply, 'sent one.' However, the term acquired a broader meaning during the time of the Roman Empire. In those days, apostles were military generals who were chosen and sent as official emissaries from a government or an empire to conquer a new territory. After gaining victory over a region and its people, one of the generals' assignments was to teach the conquered people the language, customs, values, and ways of the conquering kingdom, the new kingdom to which those people now belonged. I believe we can look at the role of these generals in history and conclude that those who are chosen to function as apostles of God's kingdom should function in similar ways."[1]

Miracles Began in the Marketplace

And He called the twelve to Himself, and began to send them out two by two, and gave them power over unclean spirits (Mark 6:7).

He named them in pairs (Simon and Andrew, James and John, Philip and Bartholomew) and sent them out in pairs. This is an important lesson for us to follow. There are no lone rangers. We should walk and minister in pairs whenever possible. The Bible tells us that when one prays, he or she can put one thousand (demons) to flight; but when two pray, they can put 10,000 to flight (Deuteronomy 32:30). There is a dynamic of multiplication that occurs in God's power when we come together with other believers to fulfill God's plan. Throughout the book of Acts, the apostles were sent out in twos. If you are sent out to fulfill God's plan in the marketplace, you may need another with you to see the fullness of both protection as well as power.

Jesus multiplied the loaves and fishes, walked on water, healed the sick, cast demons out of people, and raised the dead. In the gospel of John, God reveals to us that we have the power and authority to do even greater works than Jesus did.

*Most assuredly, I say to you, he who believes in Me, the works that I do he will do also; and **greater works** than these he will do because I go to My Father* (John 14:12, emphasis added).

We will do even greater works than Jesus did, but we must understand our authority. Where did Jesus and later the apostles perform the majority of the miracles? In the marketplace!

We have been given the same spiritual authority the apostles were given.

*And these signs will follow **those who believe**: In My name they will cast out demons; they will speak with new tongues; they will take up serpents; and if they drink anything deadly, it will by no means hurt them; they will lay hands on the sick, and they will recover* (Mark 16:17, emphasis added).

Does it say, "These signs will follow only your pastor?" Or does it say, "These signs will follow only your elders?" On the contrary, the Word says, "These signs will follow those who believe." If you believe in Jesus' name, you have the authority to cast out demons, speak with new tongues, take up serpents, not be hurt by drinking anything deadly, and lay hands on the sick and see them recover. Yes, that means YOU!

We have been commissioned to go out and preach the Gospel. Go out means "go out!" You shouldn't hide in a church where the saved people are, but you should go out into the world where the lost people are. People watch you at work and in your environment. Can they see Jesus in you? Is the power of God in your life a testimony? Remember, it's not about you but about Jesus in you.

Look at what happened in Acts. Jesus had gone to His Father. This allowed for the power of the Holy Spirit to be released upon the earth. The gathering in the upper room on the day of Pentecost brought in the fullness of that power.

*When the Day of Pentecost had fully come, **they were all with one accord in one place.** And suddenly there came a sound from heaven, as of a rushing mighty wind, and it filled the whole house where they were sitting. Then there appeared to them divided tongues, as of fire, and one sat upon each of them. And they were all filled with the Holy Spirit and began to speak with other tongues, as the Spirit gave them utterance (Acts 2:1-4, emphasis added).*

They were all in one accord. If you want to operate in the fullness of the power of Jesus, there must be unity in your group. That would include your spouse, your business partner, your ministry team, and those in authority over you at work.

On the day of Pentecost, the apostles were filled with a new level of power and anointing, and the church grew. As you are filled with a new level of power and anointing, and people see the witness in your life, your business can grow too. This is not just for leadership. It applies to anyone in the marketplace.

A friend of mine used to work for a well-known computer company. She was a programmer and was known as the "prayer lady." Many would come to her cubicle regardless of their religious background and ask for prayer. She told them that she would be happy to pray for them, but she would pray in Jesus' name. Many were healed and delivered during those times of prayer. More importantly, Jesus was exalted. It was obvious that the God of the Trinity brought the miracles. When God moved her out of her assignment, she was one of the company's top programmers in both pay and position. She said that her reward was not about the money or the position; it was about God's glory. She was obedient to what God called her to do.

If you want God to transform you and your marketplace, pray the following prayer:

Lord, touch me while I read this book. I want to see Your face. I want to please You and fulfill all that You have for me and my business or assignment in the marketplace. Help me to understand what it will take to operate in the fullness in which Your apostles were released to operate. Show me my sin. Show me my unbelief. Show me every part of my life that is holding me back. Lord, expose my business and business practices. Let me operate in Your truth and in Your light. I pray that every aspect of my life would be available to You for Your purpose and Your glory. Lord, let the world see Your light in me and in my business. In Jesus' name, amen.

CHAPTER 2

Is Your Business
Built on an Ungodly Foundation?

One day I asked the Lord, "Why are we not seeing the miracles in the marketplace like the apostles did throughout the book of Acts?" And He responded, "You have been brought up in and taught the system of the world. This is the foundation that you have established your businesses upon, and you have asked Me to bless them. How can I fully bless structures built with ungodly foundations—Babylonian foundations?" Astonished, I wept and responded, "Lord, please show me what you mean and help me to understand."

He began by showing me that the current hierarchical system of the world found in most businesses is the system of Babylon. This is the system of pyramid-structured, self-seeking management, which originated in Babylon. This is an example of the sins of selfishness, greed, and an "I will take what I want regardless of who it hurts" attitude.

God then took me to Revelation 18:4-5,

Come out of her [Babylon], *my people, lest you share in her sins, and lest you receive of her plagues. For her sins have reached to heaven, and God has remembered her iniquities.*

God is calling us out of Babylon.

The kings [businessmen] *of the earth who committed fornication and lived luxuriously with her will weep and lament for her, when they see the smoke of her burning, standing at a distance for fear of her torment, saying, "Alas, alas, that great city Babylon, that mighty city! For in one hour your judgment has come"* (Revelation 18:9-10).

This was a clear warning. There is a time coming when God will test and judge our businesses. They must be established on godly foundations to endure this testing.

*And the merchants of the earth will weep and mourn over her, for no one buys their merchandise anymore: merchandise of gold and silver, precious stones and pearls, fine linen and purple, silk and scarlet, every kind of citron wood, every kind of object of ivory, every kind of object of most precious wood, bronze, iron, and marble; and cinnamon and incense, fragrant oil and frankincense, wine and oil, fine flour and wheat, cattle and sheep, horses and chariots, and **bodies and souls of men*** (Revelation 18:11-13, emphasis added).

In this Scripture, God is addressing all merchandising known to man at that time. He even addresses the slave trade when referencing "bodies and souls of men." Slavery will be covered in a later chapter.

The fruit that your soul longed for has gone from you, and all the things which are rich and splendid have gone from you, and you shall find them no more at all. The merchants of these things, who became rich by her, will stand at a distance for fear of her torment, weeping and wailing, and saying, "Alas, alas, that great city that was clothed in fine linen, purple, and scarlet, and adorned with gold and precious stones and pearls! For in one hour such great riches came to nothing" (Revelation 18:14-17).

Here, God is addressing issues beyond business and commerce.

He is addressing issues of the heart. They were emotionally attached to their riches, finery, and "stuff." Their souls longed for the stuff, not God. There is nothing wrong with nice, beautiful things. But when you begin to build your business for the stuff and not for God, the stuff becomes your god. Your identity and self-worth become wrapped up in your purchasing power and business influence instead of God.

*They threw dust on their heads and cried out, weeping and wailing, and saying, "Alas, alas, that great city, in which all who had ships on the sea became rich by her wealth! For in one hour she is **made desolate*** (Revelation 18:19, emphasis added).

During this coming time when God tests and judges our structures, that which is of God will be purified and strengthened, but that which is not will be "made desolate."

My next question to God was, "Lord, when and where did the Babylonian foundations begin? Where is the root? He then brought me to the book of Genesis—a good place to start!

Then Cain went out from the presence of the Lord and dwelt in the land of Nod on the east of Eden. And Cain knew his wife, and she conceived and bore Enoch. And he built a city, and called the name of the city after the name of his son—Enoch (Genesis 4:16-17).

Cain left the presence of the Lord. That is, he rebelled against God and left. He took a wife and built a city. This is the first time in Scripture that a city is mentioned. Ancient cities were not formed over an extended period of time. Instead, the people of an established area would come together and determine which god they chose to worship. Then a king would be chosen and certain ceremonies would take place. These ceremonies established the chosen king as a "son" of the local deity or god that they had selected to worship. They were then called the son of that god.

Demon possession took place, as this king was dedicated to the god.[1] Today we would identify this type of "religion" and "worship" as Satanism. It is very likely that it was in this manner that Cain established the first city.[2]

Now it came to pass, when men began to multiply on the face of the earth, and daughters were born to them, that the sons of God saw the daughters of men, that they were beautiful; and they took wives for themselves of all whom they chose ... My Spirit shall not strive with man forever, for he is indeed flesh... There were giants on the earth in those days, and also afterward, when the sons of God came in to the daughters of men and they bore children to them. Those were the mighty men who were of old, men of renown (Genesis 6:1-4).

The word *giant* is a Hebrew word meaning, "bully, tyrant, or tall in stature or authority." It comes from a word that means, "to cast down, to lie down, or fallen ones.[3] Some identify these giants as fallen angels or demons who bore children to the women they "came in to." Ultimately, the result brought great remorse to God. He said, "I will destroy man whom I have created from the face of the earth, both man and beast, creeping thing and birds of the air, for I am sorry that I have made them" (Genesis 6:7).

Praise God that Adam and Eve had another son, Seth (Genesis 4:25). It was through this family line that "man began to call on the name of the Lord" (Genesis 4:26).

As you read through all of the "begots" after Seth, you will find out that eight generations later, Noah was born. Noah's great, great-grandfather was the Enoch who "walked with God." This Enoch was also the only one in the Bible besides Elijah who was taken into God's presence without experiencing physical death.

*This is the genealogy of Noah. **Noah was a just man, perfect in his generations. Noah walked with God.** And Noah begot three sons: Shem, Ham, and Japheth. The earth also was corrupt before God, and* *the earth was filled with violence. So God looked upon the earth, and indeed it was corrupt; for all flesh had corrupted their way on the earth* (Genesis 6:9-12, emphasis added).

God chose Noah because He had a relationship with him. It appears that out of Noah's generations, Noah was God's perfect choice. Noah was obedient—a man who walked with God. Something happened to bring in corruption after the flood. Was there iniquity or sin somewhere in the generations of the other seven who were spared (Noah's wife, sons, or the wives of the sons)? The impurity very likely came in through Ham's wife. It is thought that she was a descendent of Cain.[4]

Again in prayer I asked, "Lord, what happened to bring back the iniquity?" He continued in Genesis.

*And Noah began to be a farmer, and he planted a vineyard. Then he drank of the wine and was drunk, and **became uncovered** in his tent. And Ham, the father of Canaan, **saw the nakedness** of his father, and told his two brothers outside. But Shem and Japheth took a garment, laid it on both their shoulders, and went backward and covered the nakedness of their father. Their faces were turned away, and they did not see their father's nakedness* (Genesis 9:20-23, emphasis added).

The words *uncovered* and *nakedness* are addressed in the same context in Leviticus 18 under the title of "Laws of Sexual Morality." This chapter addresses incest and improper sexual relations.

*None of you shall approach anyone who is near of kin to him, to **uncover his nakedness:** I am the Lord. The nakedness of your father or the nakedness of your mother you shall not **uncover*** (Leviticus 18:6, emphasis added).

"To uncover someone's nakedness is to have sexual intercourse with that person."[5]

So Noah awoke from his wine, and **knew** *what his younger son* **had done to him** (Genesis 9:24, emphasis added).

If Ham had merely looked upon him and spoke to his brothers, how would Noah have known what his son had done to him when he awoke? In addition, the word *knew* is the same word used when "Adam knew Eve" and "Cain knew his wife" representing intercourse.[6] It is very likely that sexual perversion took place in which Ham victimized his father against his will. This behavior was so heinous to Noah that he cursed Ham's son; thus resulting in a curse to his descendents, which they are still battling today.

Practically, when Noah cursed Ham's descendants, there may have been godly wisdom behind it. If Noah was aware of the self-centered, greediness of Ham's heart, Noah may have been concerned with the destruction that may come from that position of leadership. This leadership position would have been established down the family line. It may have been safer to establish a legacy of servanthood than to set up destruction in a legacy of leadership.

Then he [Noah] said: "Cursed be Canaan: a servant of servants he shall be to his brethren. And he said: Blessed be the Lord, the God of Shem, and may Canaan be his servant. May God enlarge Japheth, and may he dwell in the tents of Shem; and may Canaan be his servant" (Genesis 9:25-27).

The Bible references the curse that followed Canaan. Whereas Canaan was cursed for his father's sin, Cush and his future generations were cursed for their own sin.

The sons of Ham were Cush, Mizraim, Put, and Canaan. Cush

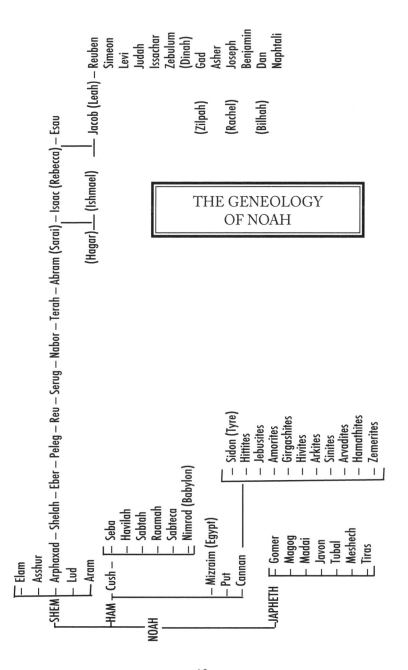

THE GENEOLOGY
OF NOAH

begot Nimrod; he began to be a mighty one on the earth. He was a mighty hunter before the Lord; therefore it is said, Like Nimrod the mighty hunter before the Lord (Genesis 10:6, 8-9).

Ham's son was named Cush. Cush's son was Nimrod. Nimrod was said to be "a mighty one and a mighty hunter before the Lord." The word *mighty* here means, "tyrant or giant."[7] It is not a word of praise but a description of arrogance. This is the same word meaning for giant, which was addressed earlier and described what brought in the wickedness of man on the earth.

And the beginning of his [Nimrod's] ***kingdom*** *was Babel, Erech, Accad, and Calneh, in the land of Shinar. From that land he went to Assyria and built Nineveh, Rehoboth, Ir, Calah, and Resen between Nineveh and Calah* (Genesis 10:10-12, emphasis added).

This is the first mention of the word *kingdom* in the Bible. Nimrod would build the first kingdom, and its name was Babel, which means "confusion." It is here in Babel, or Babylon, that Nimrod established a state religion, which included deification and worship of himself as the emperor, worship of Satan and his demons, and star worship. The deification was actually called divine kingship, which traces back to pre-flood times with Cain. He established the so-called Babylonian Mystery Religion. This religious system is described as a well-spring for all subsequent false religions.[8] This is the biblical root of Freemasonry, which I will address at great length in chapter five.

*Now the whole earth had one language and one speech. And it came to pass, as they journeyed from the east, that they found a plain in the land of Shinar, and they dwelt there. Then they said to one another, "Come, let us make bricks and bake them thoroughly." They had brick for stone, and they had asphalt for mortar. And they said, "Come. Let us build ourselves a city, and a tower whose top is in the heavens; **let*** *us make a name for ourselves, lest we be scattered abroad over the face of the whole earth"* (Genesis 11:1-4, emphasis added).

The description of the men "who made a name for themselves" is the same meaning as the "mighty men who were of old, men of renown," mentioned in Genesis 6:4. The word *renown* means "mark or memorial of individuality "[9] or men who had made a name for themselves.

Divine kingship had been reestablished. Nimrod wanted to be both a king as well as a god. Man, through his own strength, built a tower "to reach God." Note the structure: a tower or pyramid in which man sits on top. Man wanted to make a name for himself through self-exaltation. This sounds a lot like our current corporate world with its emphasis on "me, me, me," and climbing the corporate ladder.

God was obviously not pleased with this behavior and He scattered all the peoples to their respective areas.

But the Lord came down to see the city and the tower which the sons of men had built. And the Lord said, "Indeed the people are one and they all have one language, and this is what they begin to do; now nothing that they propose to do will be withheld from them. Come, let Us go down and confuse their language, that they may not understand one another's speech." So the Lord scattered them abroad from there over the face of all the earth, and they ceased building the city. Therefore its name is called Babel, because there the Lord confused the language of all the earth; and from there the Lord scattered them abroad over the face of all the earth (Genesis 11:5-9).

Could it be that in the end times, the enemy would bring the scattering back into unity through a system, which Revelation refers to as Babylon? The enemy's attempt to do this may be through trade in the world system. We are beginning to see countries coming together for the purpose of trade in the European

Union and NAFTA. We are also seeing corporations expanding their methods of doing business through outsourcing and off-shoring.

Let's look a little deeper into the life of Nimrod. Nimrod married Semiramis. She was the great Queen of Assyria.[10] Nimrod and Semiramis, as king and queen of Babylon, participated in the divine kingship processionals and were confirmed by their priests as gods named Marduk (also known as Melqart) and Astarte.[11][12]

Another name for Marduk is Bel or Baal. We find the god Bel addressed in Isaiah. Nebo is the deified name of Marduk's son.[13]

> **Bel** *bows down,* **Nebo** *stoops; their idols were on the beasts and on the* **cattle**. *Your carriages were heavily loaded, a burden to the weary beast. They stoop, they bow down together; they could not deliver the burden, but have themselves gone into captivity. Listen to Me, O house of Jacob, and all the remnant of the house of Israel, who have been upheld by Me from birth, who have been carried from the womb: Even to your old age, I am He, and even to gray hairs I will carry you! I have made, and I will bear; even I will carry, and will deliver you. To whom will you liken Me, and make Me equal and compare Me, that we should be alike? They lavish gold out of the bag, and weigh silver on the scales; they hire a goldsmith, and he makes it a god; they prostrate themselves, yes, they worship. They bear it on the shoulder, they carry it and set it in its place, and it stands; from its place it shall not move. Though one cries out to it, yet it cannot answer nor save him out of his trouble* (Isaiah 46:1-7, emphasis added).

The idols were carried on animals. Around the world today, there are still processions with idols and even individuals being carried upon men's shoulders as people lay prostrate and worship them. We also see pictures from the past with the pharaoh being carried on his throne on the shoulders of twelve men.

What does all this have to do with the marketplace or business? This is a prophetic picture of man in the position of a king sitting on top of his kingdom on the shoulders of other men. It is a picture of the king, or president of a company, literally being carried on the shoulders of all those whose hard work has lifted him up to that place of exaltation.

Let's compare this picture to that of Jesus, the Messiah, the King, coming into Jerusalem. On what did He choose to ride? A donkey. His purpose was to serve and lift up others, not to be carried and exalted.

This is the truth of Nimrod's counterfeit. It is about putting idols on animals or kings being carried on the shoulders of men. Jesus tore down the idols by saying, "Do not look at the idol but look at Me." This is what we, as CEOs and presidents of corporations, should do as well. We need to look for God's redemptive purpose in our businesses and give God all the glory instead of sitting in the top position as a king.

Let's look again at Isaiah 46:3-4.

*Listen to Me, O house of Jacob, and all the remnant of the house of Israel, who have been **upheld by Me** from birth, who have been **carried from the womb**: even to your old age, I am He, and even to gray hairs **I will carry you**! I have made, and I will bear; even **I will carry, and will deliver you*** (emphasis added).

God brings hope to us in this Scripture, because these gods of Babylon go into captivity. God will carry us and deliver us from these Babylonian gods.

Semiramis is referred to as the "Lady of Kingdoms" in Isaiah 47:5.

Sit in silence, and go into darkness, O daughter of the Chaldeans; for you shall no longer be called The Lady of Kingdoms.

Therefore hear this now, you who are given to pleasures, who dwell *securely, who say in your heart, "**I am, and there is no one else besides me**; I shall not sit as a widow, nor shall I know the loss of children;" but these two things shall come to you in a moment, in one day: the loss of children, and widowhood. They shall come upon you in their fullness because of the multitude of your sorceries, for the great abundance of your enchantments* (Isaiah 47:8-9, emphasis added).

The verses above show that Semiramis had deified herself. God is the only "I am." The vow that she spoke allowed the curses and demonic to enter. This self-exaltation brought with it the judgment of God.[14]

*For you have trusted in your wickedness; you have said, "No one sees me;" your wisdom and your knowledge have warped you; and you have said in your heart, "I am, and there is no one else besides me." Therefore evil shall come upon you; you shall not know from where it arises. And trouble shall fall upon you; you will not be able to put it off. And desolation shall come upon you suddenly, which you shall not know. Stand now with your **enchantments** and the **multitude of your sorceries**, in which you have labored from your youth – perhaps you will be able to profit, perhaps you will prevail. You are wearied in the **multitude of your counsels**; let now the **astrologers**, the **stargazers**, and the **monthly prognosticators** stand up and save you from what shall come upon you* (Isaiah 47:10-13, emphasis added).

In Revelation 18, we are looking at the same spirit. Semiramis is the Queen of Babylon.[15]

Render to her just as she rendered to you, and repay her double according to her works; in the cup which she has mixed, mix double for her. In the measure that she glorified herself and lived luxuriously, in the same measure give her torment and sorrow; for she says in her heart; "I sit as queen, and am no widow, and will not see sorrow." Therefore her plagues will come in one day – death and mourning and famine. And she will be utterly burned with fire, for strong is the Lord God who judges her (Revelation 18:6-8).

Again, self-exaltation brings the judgment of God.

In summary, if we continue to build our businesses and organizations on the same hierarchical kingship model, we set ourselves up for self-exaltation. This structure and mindset goes all the way back to the wickedness of man in the pre-flood times. This is the same Babylonian system that God is calling us out of in the end times.

Let's continue to look deeper into the inheritance that followed Ham's sons. In particular, let's look at Canaan and how the Canaanites adopted the same religious, spiritual, and cultural behavior and attitudes as the descendants of Cush.

CHAPTER 3

Is Your Business Tainted and Therefore Cursed?

The word *tainted* means, "contaminated."[1] If our business practices are contaminated, there may be spiritual consequences blocking God's blessings and breakthrough. Curses are consequences or bad outcomes. Let's go back to the book of Deuteronomy, which addresses curses. As the Israelites were delivered out of Egypt to the land of their promise, God tells them to dispossess the "ites" of the land (Deuteronomy 7). The **Hittites, Jebusites, Amorites, Girgashites, Hivites**, and **Canaanites** were all descendants of Canaan. The seventh "ites" are the **Perizzites,** which were the "ites" of Babylon. We will later see that as God was bringing the Israelites into the Promised Land, He was strongly apposed to the behavior of the Canaanites. Their behavior brought demonic oppression, curses, and judgments upon them.

The word *Canaanite* means, "to be humiliated; merchant, trafficker, trader."[2] Canaan was cursed. The sinful behavior of Ham also followed Canaan and his descendants.

God was very specific to the Israelites. He knew they would come back under the bondage of the sins that He had just freed them from if they did not obey Him.

*When the Lord your God brings you into the land which you go to possess, and has cast out many nations before you, the **Hittites**, and the **Girgashites** and the **Amorites** and the **Canaanites** and the*

21

Perizzites and the Hivites and the Jebusites, seven nations greater and mightier than you, and when the Lord your God delivers them over to you, you shall conquer them and utterly destroy them. You shall make no covenant with them nor show mercy to them. Nor shall you make marriages with them. You shall not give your daughter to their son, nor take their daughter for your son. For they will turn your sons away from following Me, to serve other gods; so the anger of the Lord will be aroused against you and destroy you suddenly. Thus you shall deal with them: you shall destroy their altars, and break down their sacred pillars, and cut down their wooden images, and burn their carved images with fire (Deuteronomy 7:1-5, emphasis added).

God told them to cast out the Hittites, Girgashites, Amorites, Canaanites, Perizzites, Hivites, and the Jebusites. When God addressed destroying their altars, sacred pillars, wooden, and carved images, He was addressing their worship of the Canaanite gods Baal and Ashtoreth. These gods are also known as Marduk and Astarte in Babylon or Osiris and Isis in Egypt. God showed His mercy because He knew the vulnerability to worship these gods was in their bloodline. He wanted to bless them abundantly by giving them this land of milk and honey while also maintaining their freedom.

Then it shall come to pass, because you listen to these judgments, and keep and do them, that the Lord your God will keep with you the covenant and the mercy which He swore to your fathers. And He will love you and bless you and multiply you; He will also bless the fruit of your womb and the fruit of your land, your grain and your new wine and your oil, the increase of your cattle and the offspring of your flock, in the land of which He swore to your fathers to give you. You shall be blessed above all peoples; there shall not be a male or female barren among you or among your livestock. And the Lord will take away from you all sickness, and will afflict you with none of the terrible dis-

eases of Egypt which you have known, but will lay them on all those
who hate you. Also you shall destroy all the peoples whom the Lord
your God delivers over to you; your eye shall have no pity on them;
nor shall you serve their gods, for that will be a snare to you
(Deuteronomy 7:12-16, emphasis added).

God gave His children a specific strategy to claim the land and
keep it for His purpose. God would fight the battles for them. His
next instructions were to march around Jericho seven times. This
specific battle plan was to take down the principality of divine
kingship in which the inhabitants of Jericho participated.[3] God's
battle plan reversed the ritual procession that the people of Jericho
marched in establishing their king as a god.[4] The people of Jericho
also worshiped Baal and Ashtoreth.[5]

After the Israelites defeated Jericho, they progressed to attack
Ai. This time the Israelites were defeated. When Joshua asked the
Lord why, Joshua was told that the Israelites had taken some of the
cursed items from Jericho and therefore Israel "could not stand before their enemies" (Joshua 7:12). It was determined that a man
named Achan was responsible. The cursed garment that Achan
stole was a Babylonian garment. This could be another indicator of
Jericho's connection to the Babylonian culture.

Indeed I [Achan] have sinned against the Lord God of Israel, and
*this is what I have done: When I saw among the spoils a **beautiful***
***Babylonian garment**, two hundred shekels of silver, and a wedge of*
gold weighing fifty shekels, I coveted them and took them. And there
they are, hidden in the earth in the midst of my tent, with the silver
under it (Joshua 7:21, emphasis added).

God had warned the Israelites about coveting the silver and
gold of those He told them to destroy. Even though the Israelites
may not have understood why they could not keep the spoils, they
learned that they could not win the battles without being obedient

to God. These objects would bring curses to them. They could not defeat Ai until the curse was broken.

> *He will deliver their kings into your hand, and you will destroy their name from under heaven; no one shall be able to stand against you until you have destroyed them. You shall burn the carved images of their gods with fire; you shall not covet the silver or gold that is on them, nor take it for yourselves, lest you be snared by it; for it is an abomination to the Lord your God.* **Nor shall you bring an abomination into your house, lest you be doomed to destruction like it.** *You shall utterly detest it and utterly abhor it, for* **it is an accursed thing** (Deuteronomy 7:24-26, emphasis added).

God told the Israelites to dispossess all of the "ites" on the land because it would be dangerous for them to come under their influence.

In Leviticus, God gave laws to Moses, which defined holy living for the Israelites' welfare and marked them out as a people separated to God. Just as He wants holiness in our lives, God wants holiness in our businesses. In Leviticus, He discourages all behavior that resembles the Canaanite pagan practices. Being separated was for their protection. God knew how vulnerable the Israelites were to being entrapped by the gods of Canaan, which were actually the same gods their ancestors were in bondage to in Babylon.

> *You shall therefore keep all My statues and all my judgments, and perform them, that the land where I am bringing you to dwell may not vomit you out. And you shall not walk in the statutes of the nation which I am casting out before you; for they commit all these things, and therefore I abhor them. But I have said to you, "You shall inherit their land, and I will give it to you to possess, a land flowing with milk and honey." I am the Lord your God, who has separated you from the peoples. You shall therefore distinguish between clean*

*animals and unclean, between unclean birds and clean, and you shall not make yourselves abominable by beast or by bird, or by any kind of living thing that creeps on the ground, which have separated from you as unclean. **And you shall be holy to Me, for I the Lord am holy, and have separated you from the peoples, that you should be Mine*** (Leviticus 20:22-26, emphasis added).

The instructions given in Leviticus 20 preceding these verses address abortion (v. 2), approaching mediums and familiar spirits (v. 6), cursing parents (v. 9), adultery (v. 10), and sexual immorality (vv. 11-16). All of these behaviors are directly or indirectly related to greed and perversion. These are Canaanite behaviors, which God abhors. They are also worldly behaviors that we see today, which God still abhors. He wants His people set apart so they won't be influenced by these practices.

Leviticus 19 and 20 address the holiness code; that is, the code for moral living. Note the word *holy* means "set apart." I once heard a well-known leadership speaker say, "There are no business ethics. Ethics are ethics." This is what God would say as well. Appropriate business conduct is addressed in the middle of other appropriate social conduct. Most of these commands promote being generous and pure. God shows His generous and benevolent nature and encourages the Israelites to behave the same. This is a sharp contrast to the gods of the land who are harsh taskmasters requiring blood, infant sacrifice, and other detestable misconduct.

God commands us in His Word to abide by the following code of conduct:

Taking care of the poor:

When you reap the harvest of your land, you shall not wholly reap the corners of your field, nor shall you gather the gleanings of your harvest. And you shall not glean your vineyard, nor shall you gather every grape of your vineyard; you shall leave them for the poor and the stranger: I am the Lord your God (Leviticus 19:9-10).

Integrity:

You shall not cheat your neighbor, nor rob him. The wages of him who is hired shall not remain with you all night until morning. You shall not curse the deaf, nor put a stumbling block before the blind, but shall fear your God: I am the Lord (Leviticus 19:13-14).

Expectations for business maturity:

When you come into the land, and have planted all kinds of trees for food, then you shall count their fruit as uncircumcised. Three years it shall be as uncircumcised to you. It shall not be eaten. But in the fourth year all its fruit shall be holy, a praise to the Lord. And in the fifth year you may eat its fruit, that it may yield to you its increase: I am the Lord your God (Leviticus 19:23-25).

Honesty:

You shall do no injustice in judgment, in measurement of length, weight, or volume. You shall have honest scales, honest weights, and honest ephah, and an honest hin: I am the Lord your God, who brought you out of the land of Egypt (Leviticus 19:35-36).

Godly economic system:

And you shall count seven Sabbaths of years for yourself, seven times seven years; and the time of the seven Sabbaths of years shall be to you forty-nine years. Then you shall cause the trumpet of the Jubilee to sound on the tenth day of the seventh month; on the Day of Atonement you shall make the trumpet to sound throughout all your land. And you shall consecrate the fiftieth year, and proclaim liberty throughout all the land to all its inhabitants. It shall be a jubilee for you; and each of you shall return to his possession, and each of you shall return to his family (Leviticus 25:8-10).

Therefore you shall not oppress one another, but you shall fear your God; for I am the Lord your God (Leviticus 25:17).

So you shall observe My statutes and keep My judgments, and perform them; and you will dwell in the land in safety. Then the land will yield its fruit, and you will eat your fill, and dwell there in safety. And if you say, "What shall we eat in the seventh year, since we shall not sow or gather in our produce?" Then I will command My blessing on you in the sixth year, and it will bring forth produce enough for three years. And you shall sow in the eighth year and eat old produce until the ninth year; until its produce comes in, you shall eat of the old harvest (Leviticus 25:18-22).

"The Jubilee was a form of socio-economic engineering. It prevented generational poverty, and made the establishment of large monopolies impossible."[6] God, in His infinite wisdom, had established an economic system which, if followed, would keep the economy stable and minimize anyone from falling into the bondage and cycle of debt and bankruptcy. It would also keep stability in the finances of the nation. The Jubilee, therefore, kept the Jews from falling deeply into bondage financially. Today, most Americans have a large amount of debt through mortgages and credit cards, which puts them in strong financial bondage. God's plan is to keep us out of debt.

The Israelites didn't follow God's strategy to be separate. They established their system of finance and trade on the one practiced by the Canaanites. This went completely against what God told them to do. They were to dispossess the "ites." Israel did not follow God's plan. They intermarried, traded with, and followed the practices of the inhabitants of the land. God would not bring them prosperity because they were not walking in obedience. In fact, their disobedience activated all of the curses addressed in Deuteronomy 28.

But it shall come to pass, if you do not obey the voice of the Lord your God, to observe carefully all His commandments and His statutes which I command you today, that all these curses will come upon you and overtake you: Cursed shall you be in the city, and cursed shall you be in the country. Cursed shall be your basket and your kneading bowl. Cursed shall be the fruit of your body and the produce of your land, the increase of your cattle and the offspring of your flocks. Cursed shall you be when you come in and cursed shall you be when you go out. The Lord will send on you cursing, confusion, and rebuke in all that you set your hand to do, until you are destroyed and until you perish quickly, because of the wickedness of your doings in which you have forsaken Me. The Lord will make the plague cling to you until He has consumed you from the land which you are going to possess. The Lord will strike you with consumption, with fever, with inflammation, with severe burning fever, with the sword, with scorching, and with mildew; they shall pursue you until you perish. And your heavens which are over your head shall be bronze, and the earth which is under you shall be iron. The Lord will change the rain of your land to powder and dust; from the heaven it shall come down on you until you are destroyed (Deuteronomy 28:15-24).

A nation whom you have not known shall eat the fruit of your land and the produce of your labor, and you shall be only oppressed and crushed continually. So you shall be driven mad because of the sight which your eyes see. The Lord will strike you in the knees and on the legs with severe boils which cannot be healed, and from the sole of your foot to the top of your head (Deuteronomy 28:33-35).

You shall carry much seed out to the field but gather little in, for the locust shall consume it. You shall plant vineyards and tend them, but you shall neither drink of the wine nor gather the grapes; for the worms shall eat them. You shall have olive trees throughout all your territory, but you shall not anoint yourself with the oil; for your olives shall drop off (Deuteronomy 28:38-40).

The alien who is among you shall rise higher and higher above you, and you shall come down lower and lower. He shall lend to you, but you shall not lend to him; he shall be the head, and you shall be the tail (Deuteronomy 28:43-44).

It is interesting to note that the majority of curses affect either your health or your finances. It appears that this may be a direct connection to purity/perversion and generosity/greed. This principle holds true today. God will not bless us when we are not following His ways.

Therefore whoever hears these sayings of Mine, and does them, I will liken him to a wise man who built his house on the rock: and the rain descended, the floods came, and the winds blew and beat on that house; and it did not fall, for it was founded on the rock. But everyone who hears these sayings of Mine, and does not do them, will be like a foolish man who built his house on the sand: and the rain descended, the floods came, and the winds blew and beat on that house, and it fell. And great was its fall (Matthew 7:24-27).

Foundations are critical. How can we build upon an ungodly business structure or foundation and expect God to honor and bless it? Marketplace teachings thus far have been taking the world systems and attempting to build upon them. If we want to see the fullness of God's kingdom in the marketplace, we need to establish godly foundations upon which to build. This is not new. The Israelites themselves established their foundations on the principles of those they were supposed to dispossess. This process brought them back into bondage.

CHAPTER 4

The Babylonian Religious
System in Israel

The Israelites had a plan for prosperity. To be like everybody else, they wanted a king. They wanted the perceived prosperity of the other nations and cried out, "God, give us a king!" The Israelites were in rebellion; therefore, God was withholding their prosperity.

Then all the elders of Israel gathered together and came to Samuel at Ramah, and said to him, "Look, you are old, and your sons do not walk in your ways. Now make us a king to judge us like all the nations." But the thing displeased Samuel when they said, "Give us a king to judge us." So Samuel prayed to the Lord. And the Lord said to Samuel, "Heed the voice of the people in all that they say to you; for they have not rejected you, but they have rejected Me, that I should not reign over them" (1 Samuel 8:4-7).

Samuel was so displeased because he knew God's heart.

*So Samuel told all the words of the Lord to the people who asked him for a king. And he said, "This will be the behavior of the king who will reign over you: **He will take your sons** and appoint them for his own chariots and to be his horsemen, and some will run before his chariots. He will appoint captains over his thousands and captains over his fifties, will set some to plow his ground and reap his harvest,*

31

and some to make his weapons of war and equipment for his chariots.
He will take your daughters *to be perfumers, cooks, and bakers.* **And**
he will take the best of your fields, your vineyards, and your olive
groves, *and give them to his servants.* **He will take a tenth** *of your*
grain and your vintage, and give it to his officers and servants. **And**
he will take your male servants, your female servants, your finest
young men, and your donkeys, and put them to his work. He will
take a tenth of your sheep. And you will be his servants. *And you*
will cry out in that day because of your king whom you have chosen
for yourselves, and the Lord will not hear you in that day" (1 Samuel
8:10-18, emphasis added).

Samuel was warning them that a king would establish slavery
and taxation, but the people did not care. They wanted a king. God
answered their request and gave them Saul.

In the process of learning how to be a king, Saul was tested to
see if he was a man after God's own heart. Would he be obedient?
Would he continue to serve the one and only God? Saul had a
choice to make. Obviously, he made the wrong choice. Perhaps it
was this decision that opened Saul up to the spirit of divine kingship.

And Samuel said, "What have you done?" Saul said, "When I saw
that the people were scattered from me, and that you did not come
within the days appointed, and that the Philistines gathered together
at Michmash, then I said, 'The Philistines will now come down on
me at Gilgal, and I have not made supplication to the Lord.'
Therefore, I felt compelled, and offered a burnt offering." And Samuel
said to Saul, "You have done foolishly. **You have not kept the com-**
mandment of the Lord your God, which He commanded you. *For*
now the Lord would have established your kingdom over Israel for-
ever. But now your kingdom shall not continue. The Lord has sought
for Himself a man after His own heart, and the Lord has commanded
him to be a commander over His people, because you have not kept

what the Lord commanded you" (1 Samuel 13:11-14, emphasis added).

Saul acted as both king and priest. It was not his role to make the sacrifice. This was his first step toward letting in the spirit of divine kingship. The next step is when he established a monument for himself.

Now the word of the Lord came to Samuel, saying, "I greatly regret that I have set up Saul as king, for he has turned back from following Me, and has not performed My commandments." And it grieved Samuel, and he cried out to the Lord all night. So when Samuel rose early in the morning to meet Saul, it was told Samuel, saying, "Saul went to Carmel, and indeed, he set up a monument for himself; and he has gone on around, passed by, and gone down to Gilgal" (1 Samuel 15:10-12, emphasis added).

Why would it be so important for Samuel to be aware of this behavior if it meant nothing? Saul established a monument for himself. The word for monument is the word *yad*, which means "a hand, strength, or power." It is also the word for *phallus*.[1][2] Establishing a monument representing a phallus was very likely introduced in Egypt or from the Canaanites who participated in Babylonian culture. Next, Saul has "gone on around." The word for this is *sabab*, which means "to turn, to be brought around." It also means, "to march or walk around."[3] Could this have actually been a marching around as in the procession of divine kingship? The word for "passed by" is *abar*. It means, "to pass over or cross over or to dedicate."[4] Was this actually a process to become a false god and allowing demon possession? Was it here that Saul dedicated himself to Satan and turned his heart from the Lord? Finally, the word for "gone down" is *yarad*, which means "to descend, decline, to lay prostrated."[5] Saul lay prostrated in Gilgal.

All their wickedness is in Gilgal, for there I hated them. Because of the evil of their deeds I will drive them from My house; I will love them no more. All their princes are rebellious (Hosea 9:15).

"Gilgal had become a center of idolatry."[6] Gilgal was also the place that the Israelites went through corporate circumcision (see Joshua 5:9). Could the enemy have taken the purity, self-denial, and sacrifice of circumcision and perverted it to self-exaltation and idolatry?

These Scriptures could be translated that Saul went to Carmel and set up a phallus or obelisk to himself—taking the glory for defeating the Amalekites. He then marched around this obelisk and performed the procession and ritual required to establish divinity. He actually crossed over to the other side by dedicating himself to Satan, and then lay prostrate to worship in Gilgal, the center of idolatry. This perspective would explain why God told Samuel that Saul turned his back from following Him, which caused God to reject Saul as king.

But the Spirit of the Lord departed from Saul, and a distressing spirit from the Lord troubled him (1 Samuel 16:14).

It was David who played the harp to bring spiritual peace to Saul. The curse that followed Saul was delusion followed by suicide. History shows us examples of other leaders who were delusional and ended their lives in suicide. Some examples include Alexander the Great, Nero, Hitler, and Stalin. This is the curse that follows self-exaltation and divine kingship.

Saul lost his throne. David was anointed to be the next king. He was a man after God's own heart. The enemy could not get to David in obvious ways, so he came after David through a new direction—his business associates.

*Now **Hiram King of Tyre** sent messengers to David, and cedar trees, with masons and carpenters, to build him a house. So David knew that the Lord had established him as king over Israel, for his kingdom was highly exalted for the sake of His people Israel. **Then David took more wives** in Jerusalem, and David begot more sons and daughters* (1 Chronicles 14:1-3, emphasis added).

If an individual is called to business, the spirit of Freemasonry will attempt to come after his/her gifting. The king of Tyre represents self-exaltation, divine kingship, and Freemasonry. I will further elaborate on this point later in the chapter.

It is interesting that David took more wives after the establishment of his relationship with the king of Tyre. The Ten Commandments forbid adultery. However, this was a popular social and political practice for kings at the time to establish alliances with other kingdoms and nations. This is another example of how the Israelites adopted behaviors of the "ites" and Babylonians. "Ancient kings frequently undertook multiple marriages for political reasons—a king would marry the daughter of another king in order to create a stronger alliance. The larger a king's harem, the more prestige the king enjoyed."[7]

After David left the throne, Hiram, the king of Tyre, had even more influence on Solomon.

Then Solomon sent to Hiram King of Tyre, saying: "As you have dealt with David my father, and sent him cedars to build himself a house to dwell in, so deal with me" (2 Chronicles 2:3).

And Hiram answered saying,

*And now I have sent a skillful man, **endowed with understanding**, Hiram my master craftsman* (2 Chronicles 2:13, emphasis added).

This skillful man is the man referred to as Hiram Abiff, who was the central figure in the rituals of modern day Freemasonry. His "understanding" was not godly wisdom but enlightenment or illumination from the Babylonian Mystery Religions. This illumination is sought by all Masons as they climb new levels and degrees.[8] God had blessed Solomon with wisdom. In fact, God made Solomon "wiser than all men" (1 Kings 4:31). Why then did Solomon need this man Hiram to bring him understanding? Solomon also began to rebel against God at this time by practicing polygamy as his father David had done. As he followed after the gods of his many wives, this practice turned Solomon's heart away from God.

> *But King Solomon loved many foreign women, as well as the daughter of* **Pharaoh**: *women of the* **Moabites, Ammonites, Edomites, Sidonians,** *and* **Hittites**—*from the nations of whom the Lord had said, to the children of Israel,* **You shall not intermarry with them, nor they with you.** *Surely they will turn away your hearts after their gods. Solomon clung to these in love. And he had seven hundred wives, princesses, and three hundred concubines; and his wives turned away his heart. For it was so, when Solomon was old, that his wives turned his heart after other gods; and his heart was not loyal to the Lord his God, as was the heart of his father David. For Solomon went after* **Ashtoreth** *the goddess of the Sidonians, and after* **Milcom** *the Abomination of the Ammonites. Solomon did evil in the sight of the Lord, and did not fully follow the Lord, as did his father David. Then Solomon built a high place for* **Chemosh** *the abomination of Moab, on the hill that is east of Jerusalem, and for* **Molech** *the abomination of the people of Ammon. And he did likewise for all his foreign wives, who burned incense and sacrificed to their gods* (1 Kings 11:1-8, emphasis added).

Solomon opened the door to the gods that the Israelites had left when they escaped Egypt. Ashtoreth was the Sidonian goddess of fertility. This is the same goddess known as Astarte by the

Canaanites, Semiramis by the Babylonians, and Isis by the Egyptians. Milcom was the god of the Ammonites. This is the same god known as Marduk by the Canaanites, Nimrod by the Babylonians, and Osiris by the Egyptians. Chemosh was the god of the Moabites. The Moabites were the tribe who came from the incestuous relationship between Lot and his daughter. Molech is the god of the Ammonites involving infant sacrifice.[9] This is the same spirit behind abortion.

Samuel had cautioned the Israelites that a king would tax the people (1 Samuel 8:10-17). Taxation was a practice that the kings of the other nations enforced upon the people to increase their wealth. The Bible first mentions it in Genesis 47:24, "And it shall come to pass in the harvest that you shall give one-fifth to Pharaoh." This was established in Egypt. Taxation is reintroduced to Israel during Solomon's reign to pay for his palace and the temple. Even though he was the wealthiest man in the world, Solomon needed to raise additional finances. Hiram influenced Solomon to establish taxation as a means to pay his workmen. This socio-political practice eventually caused the division that separated Israel and Judah.[10] Note, I am not suggesting the elimination of taxes. Taxation is a biblical principle; however, this was an example where it led to abuse and eventually the division of a nation.

Samuel also cautioned the Israelites that a king would institute slavery (1 Samuel 8:10-18). Solomon and the king of Tyre made a treaty or contract to build the temple. They needed a large workforce to facilitate this project, and Solomon raised up forced labor out of Israel (1 Kings 5:13).[11] The people became resentful of the heavy yoke placed upon them, which brought further division to Solomon's kingdom (1 Kings 12:4). Slavery is another by-product of kingship that occurred with the king of Tyre. Wherever there are slave masters, there are slaves.[12]

As Solomon continued to adhere to the influences of Hiram, he reintroduced Israel to the spirits of Babylon and Egypt. These are the spirits of Freemasonry that I will cover in chapter five. As we read further in First Kings, we find that most of the later kings of both Israel and Judah worshipped the gods of the "ites," and their business alliances continued to strengthen with Tyre and Sidon. When Hiram of Tyre built the temple, he also brought in his understanding of the Babylonian Mystery Religion. In this process, Freemasonry was brought into and established in Solomon's temple.

*The Spirit lifted me up between earth and heaven, and brought me in visions of God to Jerusalem, to the door of the north gate of the **inner court**, where the seat of the **image of jealousy** was, which **provokes to jealousy**. And behold, the glory of the God of Israel was there, like the vision that I saw in the plain. Then He said to me, "Son of man, lift your eyes now toward the north." So I lifted my eyes toward the north, and there, north of the altar gate, was this **image of jealousy** in the entrance* (Ezekiel 8:3-5, emphasis added).

When we participate in idolatry, we provoke God to jealousy. God was showing Ezekiel that an early form of Freemasonry was being practiced in the temple. Solomon let it in through Hiram, and it was the curse that brought the Israelites into captivity to Babylon. They found themselves back in slavery underneath Cush (Babylon) through their relationship with Tyre (Canaan).

*Furthermore He said to me, "Son of man, do you see what they are doing, the **great abominations that the house of Israel commits here, to make Me go far away from My sanctuary?** Now turn again, you will see greater abominations." So He brought me to the door of the court; and when I looked, there was a hole in the wall. Then He said to me, "Son of man, dig into the wall," and when I dug into the wall, there was a door. And He said to me, "Go in, and see the wicked abominations which they are doing there." So I went in and saw, and there – every sort of creeping thing, abominable beasts, and all the idols of the house of Israel, portrayed all around on the walls. And* *there stood before them **seventy men of the elders of the house of Israel**, and in their midst stood Jaazaniah the son of Shaphan. Each man had a censer in his hand, and a thick cloud of incense went up. Then He said to me, "Son of man, have you seen what the elders of the house of Israel do in the dark, every man in the room of his idols? For they say, 'The Lord does not see us, the Lord has forsaken the land.'"* (Ezekiel 8:6-12, emphasis added).

The elders of the church were participating in a ritual practiced by Freemasons today. They operated in secret and thought that the Lord did not see them. The elders were also participating in idolatry. This specifically came against the commandments and opened them up to a multitude of curses.

*And He said to me, "Turn again, and you will see greater abominations that they are doing." So He brought me to the door of the north gate of the Lord's house; and to my dismay, women were sitting there **weeping for Tammuz*** (Ezekiel 8:13-14, emphasis added).

Tammuz is a Babylonian god of seasons, also known as a fertility god.[13] His consort is Ishtar. This is another pair like Osiris and Isis. In fact, Ishtar is the same spirit as Isis in a different culture. In addition, Ishtar means, "Eastern Star." Her symbol is a pentagram, which is also the symbol for the Order of the Eastern Star, the women's Masonic organization.[14]

*Then He said to me, "Have you seen this, O son of man? Turn again, you will see greater abominations than these." So He brought me into **the inner court of the Lord's house**; and there, at the door of the temple of the Lord, between the porch and the altar, were about twenty-five men with their backs toward the temple of the Lord and their faces toward the east, and they were **worshiping the sun toward the east*** (Ezekiel 8:15-16, emphasis added).

This is blatant worship of Osiris, the sun god.

*And He said to me, "Have you seen this, O son of man? Is it a trivial thing to the house of Judah to commit the abominations which they commit here? For they have filled the land with violence; then they have returned to provoke Me to anger. Indeed they **put the branch to their nose**"* (Ezekiel 8:17, emphasis added).

The acacia branch is put to one's nose during Masonic rituals. It is also part of the Masonic burial ceremony.[15]

God responds to the idolatry. The glory of the Lord leaves the temple.

Therefore I also will act in fury. My eye will not spare nor will I have pity; and though they cry in My ears with a loud voice, I will not hear them (Ezekiel 9:18).

Then the glory of the Lord departed from the threshold of the temple and stood over the cherubim. And the cherubim lifted their wings and mounted up from the earth in my sight. When they went out, the wheels were beside them; and they stood at the door of the east gate of the Lord's house, and the glory of the God of Israel was above them (Ezekiel 10:18-19).

God leaves the temple because the leadership was participating in rituals that foreshadowed modern day Freemasonry. Ezekiel 23 addresses Israel and Judah's harlotry in going after the ways of the world spiritually, politically, and socially. The Israelites worshiped the false gods and followed the Babylonian trade practices.

*The word of the Lord came again to me, saying: "Son of man, there were two women, the daughters of one mother. They committed **harlotry in Egypt**, they committed harlotry in their youth; their breasts were there embraced, their virgin bosom was there pressed. Their* *names: Oholah the elder and Oholibah her sister; they were Mine, and they bore sons and daughters. As for their names, Samaria is Oholah, and Jerusalem is Oholibah. Oholah played the harlot even though she was Mine; and she lusted for her lovers, the neighboring Assyrians, who were clothed in purple, captains and rulers, all of them desirable young men, horsemen riding on horses* (Ezekiel 23:1-6, emphasis added).

God is addressing Israel and Judah after the kingdom was divided. They both made covenant, which is a business contract in today's world, with Assyria. The Assyrian Empire whose capital city was Nineveh, also established by Nimrod, included Tyre, Sidon, Babylon, and Egypt. Semiramis was the Queen of Assyria. The Israelites were again in alliance with nations who worship the Babylonian spirits Marduk and Astarte (Nimrod and Semiramis).

Thus she committed her harlotry with them, all of them choice men of Assyria; and with all for whom she lusted, with all their idols, she defiled herself. She has never given up her harlotry brought from Egypt, for in her youth they had lain with her, pressed her virgin bosom and poured out their immorality upon her (Ezekiel 23:7-8).

Israel's relationship with Assyria caused her to go into captivity again. This can happen to us as well when we go back to the ways of the world; we become of the world. Both Israel and Judah went back into bondage.

Therefore I have delivered her into the hand of her lovers, into the hand of the Assyrians, for whom she lusted. They **uncovered her** **nakedness, took away her sons and daughters,** *and slew her with the sword; she became a byword among women, for they had executed judgment on her* (Ezekiel 23:9-10, emphasis added).

Again, we are hearing the same message regarding "The Lady

of Kingdoms" in Isaiah 47 and Revelation 18. The same curse was activated.

Now although her sister Oholibah saw this, she became more corrupt in her lust than she, and in her harlotry more corrupt than her sister's harlotry (Ezekiel 23:11).

*Therefore, Oholibah, thus says the Lord God: "Behold, I will stir up your lovers against you, from whom you have alienated yourself, and I will bring them against you from every side: The **Babylonians**, all the Chaldeans, Pekod, Shoa, Koa, all the Assyrians with them, all of them desirable young men, governors and rulers, captains and men of renown, all of them riding on horses. And they shall come against you with chariots, wagons, and war-horses, with a horde of people. They shall array against you buckler, shield, and helmet all around. I will delegate judgment to them, and they shall judge you according to their judgments. I will set **My jealousy** against you, and they shall deal furiously with you; they shall remove your nose and your ears, and your remnant shall fall by the sword; **they shall take your sons and your daughters**, and your remnant shall be devoured by fire. They shall also **strip you of your clothes and take away your beautiful jewelry**. Thus I will make you cease your lewdness and your harlotry brought from the land of **Egypt**, so that you will not lift your eyes to them, nor remember Egypt anymore"* (Ezekiel 23:22-27, emphasis added).

Because Israel and Judah had opened their spiritual doors by worshiping false gods, the gods of Babylon (Egypt) and Assyria, Babylon and Assyria had the legal right, spiritually speaking, to take them back into bondage. Israel found herself in captivity again.

A few verses later, God judges Tyre and Sidon. He is clearly angry with them and gets very specific about their business practices.

I will put an end to the sound of your [Tyre's] *songs, and the sound of your harps shall be heard no more. I will make you like the top of a rock; you shall be a place for spreading nets, and you shall never be rebuilt, for I the Lord have spoken, says the Lord God. Thus says the Lord God to Tyre: "Will the coastlands not shake at the sound of your fall, when the wounded cry, when slaughter is made in the midst of you? Then all the princes of the sea will come down from their thrones, lay aside their robes, and take off their embroidered garments; they will clothe themselves with trembling; they will sit on the ground, tremble every moment, and be astonished at you"* (Ezekiel 26:13-16).

*For thus says the Lord God: "When I make you a desolate city, like cities that are not inhabited, when I bring the deep upon you, and great waters cover you, then I will bring you down with those who descend **into the Pit**, to the people of old, and I will make you dwell in the lowest part of the earth, in places desolate from antiquity, with those who go down to the **Pit**, so that you may never be inhabited; and I shall establish glory in the land of the living. I will make you a terror, and you shall be no more; though you are sought for, you will never be found again," says the Lord God* (Ezekiel 26:19-21, emphasis added).

When God is referring to the pit, He is referring to hell. Note that both Tyre and Jericho were not to be built again. God clearly does not want us to establish our business foundations on the practices of divine kingship that were used in both Tyre and Jericho. These are foundations of power, corruption, and greed with no regard for human life or salvation.

Later, God speaks to Ezekiel and tells him to prophesy to Tyre.

*Say to Tyre, "You who are situated at the entrance of the sea, **merchant** of the peoples on many coastlands, thus says the Lord God: 'O Tyre, you have said I am perfect in beauty. Your borders are in the* *midst of the seas. Your builders have perfected your beauty* (Ezekiel 27:1-4, emphasis added).

Elders of Gebal and its wise men were in you to caulk your seams; all the ships of the sea and their oarsmen were in you **to market your merchandise** (Ezekiel 27:9, emphasis added).

Tarshish was your merchant because of your many luxury goods. *They gave you silver, iron, tin and lead for your goods. Javan, Tubal, and Meshech were your traders. They* **bartered human lives** *and vessels of bronze for your merchandise* (Ezekiel 27:12-13, emphasis added).

Judah and the land of Israel were your traders. They traded for your merchandise (Ezekiel 27:17, emphasis added).

When your wares went out by sea, you satisfied many people; **you enriched the kings of the earth with your many luxury goods and your merchandise.** *But you are broken by the seas in the depths of the waters; your merchandise and the entire company will fall in your midst. All the inhabitants of the isles will be astonished at you; their kings will be greatly afraid, and their countenance will be troubled. The merchants among the peoples will hiss at you; you will become a horror, and be no more forever"* (Ezekiel 27:33-36, emphasis added).

God curses Tyre's ability to merchandise ever again. Their corruption, pride, and greed needed to be destroyed. Both Judah and Israel had established business alliances with Tyre. They were building their own kingdoms under the influence of the Canaanites, instead of God's kingdom established with godly principles. Historically, Ezekiel's prophesy was fulfilled when Tyre was destroyed by Alexander the Great in 332 BC.[16]

Finally, the Lord addresses the king of Tyre in Ezekiel 28:1-2.

Son of man, say to the prince of Tyre, Thus says the Lord God: "Because your heart is lifted up, **and you say, 'I am a god, I sit in the seat of gods.** *In the midst of the seas.' Yet you are a man, and not a god, though you set your heart as the heart of a god"* (emphasis added).

God is addressing the spirit of divine kingship. In fact, God likens the king of Tyre to Lucifer, who fell from heaven. This is the antichrist spirit.

You were the anointed cherub who covers; I established you; you were on the holy mountain of God; you walked back and forth in the midst of fiery stones. You were perfect in your ways from the day you were created, till iniquity was found in you. **By the abundance of your trading you became filled with violence within, and you sinned;** *therefore I cast you as a profane thing out of the mountain of God; and I destroyed you. O covering cherub, from the midst of the fiery stones* (Ezekiel 28:14-16, emphasis added).

Then God gives a strong word against Sidon.

Son of man, set your face toward Sidon, and prophesy against her, and say, "Thus says the Lord God: 'Behold, I am against you, O Sidon; I will be glorified in your midst; and they shall know that I am the Lord, when I execute judgments in her and am hallowed in her. For I will send pestilence upon her, and blood in her streets; the wounded shall be judged in her midst by the sword against her on every side; then they shall know that I am the Lord. And there shall no longer be a **pricking brier or a painful thorn for the house of Israel** *from among all who are around them, who despise them. Then they shall know that I am the Lord God'"* (Ezekiel 28:21-24, emphasis added).

God instructs the Israelites to drive out the inhabitants from the land they are to possess. If they do not, the inhabitants will be a constant problem and irritant to them. Furthermore, God will treat the Israelites as He would the ungodly inhabitants.

> *But if you do not drive out the inhabitants of the land from before you, then it shall be that **those whom you let remain shall be irritants in your eyes and thorns in your sides**, and they shall harass you in the land where you dwell. Moreover it shall be that I will do to you as I thought to do to them* (Numbers 33:55, emphasis added).

God dealt with the thorns by annihilating them.

You may be wondering, "What does this have to do with me and my business?" It is important to understand our enemy and his strategies if we want to have victory. Many times the enemy's assignment against the anointing for business is Freemasonry, which is the Babylonian Religious System in our world today. This may be more relevant to you than you think.

Let me share an example of the importance of breaking this curse in our personal lives in order to overcome in business. A few years ago, some elders from our church approached us for restoration ministry. They were having great difficulty in selling two farms in Kansas that had been in their family for generations. The Holy Spirit led us to delve deep into the curses and demonic spirits that had come in through Freemasonry in both family lines. This demonic stronghold had blocked their finances for years. A week following the time of ministry, they went to Kansas to auction their land. We gave them some assignments to clear the land of all Masonic curses and dedicate it to the Lord. The auctioneer told them the top figures that they could expect to receive for this sale. To everyone's amazement, the land sold for $400,000 more than the auctioneer's highest expectations. Glory to God! This couple believed very strongly that the financial breakthrough was directly related to the freedom they received through the ministry. If your finances or the finances of your business are blocked in any way, it may be the result of a Masonic curse from you or your generations.

There are many other challenges that many face both personally and in business that may also be tied to Freemasonry. This is why I am addressing it at such great length.

We as individuals need to deal with our own roots of Babylon and Freemasonry brought in through our own sin and the sin of our forefathers—whether knowingly or unknowingly. We also need to uproot it from our land and our businesses. If we have any roots of Freemasonry in our businesses, the fullness of the glory of God will not inhabit it. This is why we may lead some to the Lord, but the entirety of His signs and wonders cannot fully be manifested. Our foundations are to be built on Jesus Christ as our King.

CHAPTER 5

The Babylonian Religious System in Our World Today

I believe the enemy is attempting to ensnare us blindly through our system of trade, as he did the Israelites. Are we so entrenched in the Babylonian system that we can't even see it? As we enter the end times, we must be in a strong position. If we are entangled in the Babylonian structure and are not even able to identify it, we may completely miss our assignment from God. Even worse, we could become a casualty of the enemy because we are in the wrong place at the wrong time. There is a strengthening movement once again to bring the world together through a one world government or "One World Order." It seems that this reorganization is being introduced through finance and trade. It plays upon the greed of the nations. The European Union is passing laws regarding patents, the environment, and food, which are establishing unity throughout Europe.

We are also seeing significant changes in currency. Many of the European nations now use the Eurodollar. There is a new buzz-word, Amero, which is suggested to be replacing the American dollar, Canadian dollar, and Mexican peso.[1]

The North American Free Trade Association, or NAFTA, is breaking down the barriers to trade between the United States, Canada, and Mexico. We even hear the discussion of joining these three as one country. The Security and Prosperity Partnership (SPP) of North America was established in 2005 to begin to implement the unity of these three countries.[2] "Many SPP working groups appear to be working toward achieving specific objectives as defined by a May 2005 Council on Foreign Relations task force report, which presented a blueprint for expanding the SPP agreement into a North American Union that would merge the US, Canada and Mexico into a new governmental form."[3] The North American Super Corridor is a highway that is currently being built to join Mexico, North America, and Canada together to facilitate trade between the three countries.[4] Bit by bit, the world is coming closer together.

Are we rebuilding the Tower of Babel? God scattered all of the people and confused their language. The rebuilding of Babel requires unity—One World Order—a system where all on the earth have one language, one currency, and one religion with ultimately one king, the Antichrist.

Obviously, for the entire world to respond to this event in unity, there must be some common place of power. This source of power must include individuals of each nation with the most power as well as financial resources. The organization that could do this is the Illuminati—a hidden international power organization that backs governmental and international strategies.

What is the Illuminati? Where and when did it begin? I had a vision of the pyramid on the back of the one dollar bill. God said the top part of the pyramid lifted up with the "all-knowing" eye is the Illuminati.

The Illuminati is the top of the pyramid

The Great Seal[5]

50

of Freemasonry. It is the elite of the Secret Societies. It is the organization that is behind One World Order. It is also believed that as individuals attain the highest levels in this secret society, they will become illuminated and have achieved a higher mystical understanding of the universe.[6]

Adam Weishaupt founded the Illuminati on May 1, 1776, in Bavaria, which is in the southern part of Germany.[7] At the roots of both World Wars, we will find the Illuminati.[8] It is said that they secretly manipulate world events. Ultimately, it is about establishing One World Order where the "Order" will have ultimate control.[9] They will try to establish one monetary system, one religion, and one language. It is the Illuminati that will be behind the mark of the beast. This organization is the mastermind behind the world wealth. It controls the central banking system.[10]

The Illuminati first entered the United States through the central banking system.[11] The world of finance has connections to the Illuminati through the banking industry, insurance companies, investment firms, the stock exchange, and other large corporations. Our connection to these organizations could keep us bound to the system of Babylon. Please note that some but not all individual companies within these industries are connected to the Illuminati.

Revelation 18 addresses all forms of trade. Are we as Christians willing to begin to look at establishing a system of finance and commerce outside of the structure of Babylon (Illuminati)?

Most of us are much more familiar with Freemasonry. Whether we've inherited our grandfather's ring, seen the local Lodge while traveling through the small towns on a road trip, or watched the History Channel, we are somewhat familiar with the term and the organization. Freemasonry traces its roots all the way back to the Tower of Babel. It so permeates our western culture that we may be entangled in its influence and not even realize this connection. It is a secret society that threatens its members with personal and generational curses if they reveal any information about their craft. Even if you have never participated in it personally, chances are that your father, grandfather, or great-grandfather made vows, oaths, or dedications concerning you and your legacy.

Modern Freemasonry is a fraternal organization that began formally meeting in the early 18th century. "The first Grand Lodge was founded in London, England, in 1717."[12] Masons are known for their philanthropic activities such as building hospitals or raising money for premature infants. Many of us have seen them in the local Fourth of July Parade riding in small cars with red hats on their heads.

Examples of Masonic organizations include Blue Lodge, Scottish Rite, York Rite, Shriners, and Master Masons.[13] Other Masonic organizations include Elks, Moose, Eagles, Woodsmen of the World, Oddfellows, Buffalo, Druids, Foresters, Knights of Columbus, Knights of Pythias, DeMolay, and fraternities. Women's groups include Order of the Eastern Star, Job's Daughters, P.E.O. (Philanthropic Educational Organization), sororities, and other secretive philanthropic organizations. Mormonism has its roots in Masonic philosophy. Joseph Smith, the founder of Mormonism, was a 33rd Degree Mason.[14] Jewish Kabbalism, which is a form of Jewish Mysticism, also has its roots in Freemasonry.[15]

People are encouraged to join these organizations and told that it will help bring success to their business relationships, particularly in the worlds of finance, land, and law.[16] Many of our forefathers were Freemasons. In fact, many signed the Declaration of Independence. In addition, a number of our US presidents as well as one-third of all Supreme Court Justices throughout history were Masons. Many pastors and religious leaders are also Masons.[17]

Most people do not understand covenant. Participants of Freemasonry make a covenant with Satan. This is done through rituals and oaths. "By this degree *[Shriner—33rd Degree]* a person has attained pure Luciferian doctrine. He accepts Lucifer as God"[18] (italics mine). This nullifies any covenant with God.

You shall have no other gods before Me. You shall not make for yourself a carved image—any likeness of anything that is in heaven above, or that is in the earth beneath, or that is in the water under the earth; you shall not bow down to them nor serve them. For I, the Lord your God, am a jealous God, visiting the iniquity of the fathers upon the children to the third and fourth generations of those who hate Me (Exodus 20:3-5).

Also I say to you, whoever confesses Me before men, him the Son of Man also will confess before the angels of God. But he who denies Me before men will be denied before the angels of God. And anyone who speaks a word against the Son of Man, it will be forgiven him, but to him who blasphemes against the Holy Spirit, it will not be forgiven (Luke 12:8-12).

God made a covenant with the Israelites after freeing them from slavery in Egypt. This covenant is referred to as the Mosaic Covenant.

You have seen what I did to the Egyptians, and how I bore you on eagles' wings and brought you to Myself. Now therefore, if you will indeed obey My voice and keep My covenant, then you shall be a special treasure to Me above all people; for all the earth is Mine. And you shall be to Me a kingdom of priests and a holy nation (Exodus 19:4-6).

When we accept Christ and are born again, we are adopted into the covenant that God has made with His people. But we cannot have it both ways. In the Mosaic Covenant, God said that we would be His special treasure and that we would be a kingdom of priests to Him. Masonry teaches followers to build their own kingdom and through the process of self-exaltation, reach higher levels of enlightenment—thus building the pyramids or the Tower of Babel.

In Freemasonry, each level attained is said to bring a higher level of so-called enlightenment. The first three levels are referred to as the Blue Lodge. Level one is the initiation for the Entered Apprentice.[19] In this initiation, the initiate is dressed in pajamas with a blindfold or hoodwink placed over his eyes. This is a prophetic act, which is a physical acting out that causes a change in the spiritual. It can cause both physical and spiritual blindness in not only the initiate, but also in his family, business, and future legacy. This is a key point to understand. Most Masons do not understand the depth of the sin that they have entered into because of the spiritual blindness that results in placing this hoodwink over their eyes. Next, a noose is placed around their neck. This noose represents a "cable tow," which is also a prophetic act establishing a soul tie or spiritual tie that will keep them always controlled and manipulated by members of the Lodge. Next, their "left breast is bared and pricked with a sharp dagger or compass."[20] This establishes a blood covenant. It is a blood covenant with Satan.

The life source is in the blood. You cannot be in covenant with both God and Satan. By accepting Satan, you nullify your covenant with God. You therefore open yourself to all of the curses that come with idolatry. Because idolatry is an abomination to God, you open yourself to all curses.

> *But it shall come to pass, if you do not obey the voice of the Lord your God, to observe carefully all His commandments and His statutes which I command you today, that all these curses will come upon you and overtake you: cursed shall you be in the city, and cursed shall you be in the country. Cursed shall be your basket and your kneading bowl. Cursed shall be the fruit of your body and the produce of your land, the increase of your cattle and the offspring of your flocks. Cursed shall you be when you come in, and cursed shall you be when you go out. The Lord will send on you cursing, confusion, and rebuke in all that you set your hand to do, until you are destroyed and until you perish quickly, because of the wickedness of your doings in which you have forsaken Me* (Deuteronomy 28:15-20).

What makes the curses so devastating in Freemasonry is that not only do you open yourself and your family to the curses of Deuteronomy 28, but also because of the oaths spoken, you specifically open yourself to the ramifications of what will come against you and your family if you break the covenant made with Satan.

During this level one process, the initiate's "left arm and knee are made bare." This represents being half bare or half covered. "The shoes are removed and the right foot wears a slipshod slipper." This ritual removes the armor of God (Ephesians 6:10-20) and replaces it with false armor. The candidate next is told that he is the "cornerstone."[21] Who is the Chief Cornerstone? Jesus Christ is the Chief Cornerstone (Ephesians 2:20). The following oath is spoken: "All of this I most solemnly, sincerely promise and swear . . . binding myself under no less penalty than that of having my throat slit from ear to ear, my tongue torn out from its roots, and my body buried in the sands of the sea at low water mark . . . should I ever knowingly violate this my Entered Apprentice obligation. So help me God."[22]

Some of the curses invoked through this initiation manifest as follows: asthma, throat disorders, cancer of the mouth, speech disorders, autism, cleft palate, silence, injury to the mouth or throat, being cut violently in surgery to the throat or mouth, sinus problems, respiratory problems, cutthroat business dealings, beheading, loss of speech, sorcery, and witchcraft.[23]

The second level of the Blue Lodge is called the Ceremony of Passing Fellowcraft. The initiate is dressed the same except the right side is exposed. The cable tow is "wrapped around the right shoulder twice," which is another prophetic act of making covenant. The oath spoken is as follows: ". . . the left breast being torn open and the heart plucked out and given to the fowls of the air or the devouring beasts of the field as prey." Some of the curses brought in at this level manifest as follows: witchcraft, cardiac failure, cardiovascular failure, heart attack, being shot or stabbed in the heart, breast cancer, premature death, injustice, seeking intelligence and knowledge from man not God. [24]

The third level is the raising of the Master Mason. At this level, both arms are bare, both knees are bare, and feet are slipshod or bare. The cable tow is wrapped around the body of the candidate and dragging behind him.[25] The soul tie or spiritual tie has been further established where the initiate can no longer break free of the connection to the Lodge. There is a ritual, which reenacts the death of Hiram Abiff, which mocks the death and resurrection of Jesus Christ.[26] This ceremony also represents the death and resurrection of Osiris (Marduk, Nimrod). The oath spoken during this ritual is as follows: "...my heart and other vital organs be removed and thrown over the left shoulder and carried into the valley of Jehoshaphat to be devoured by fowls of the air...binding myself, under no less penalty than that of having my body severed in two, my bowels torn out, burnt to ashes and the ashes scattered to the four cardinal points of heaven so that there is no trace of remembrance of being left among men."[27] It is at this level that the Mason receives his first covenant ring.[28] Accepting this ring brings a curse of divorce into your marriage. It will never allow true godly unity in a family. Additional curses evoked include: death, murder, violence, all of the Egyptian gods (demons), false martyrdom, stroke, blood hemorrhage, migraines, headaches, vision impairment, blindness, concussion, brain damage, obsession with death, suicide, self-destruction, anorexia, bulimia, death by hanging, bowel cancer, stomach cancer, death by fire, false light (Lucifer), hydra spirit, medium spirit, false signs and wonders, and divination.[29]

Following the Blue Lodge, the initiate chooses between the York Rite or the Scottish Rite as he continues his process of "enlightenment." The York Rite goes from level four through ten. The top level is a Knight's Templar. The Scottish Rite goes from level four through thirty-three. The top level or degree is a Shriner. The legend of Hiram Abiff continues throughout both rites.

At the top level, Baphomet is worshipped.[30] Baphomet is the god of both Satanists and Freemasons. As presented on a Satanist website, Baphomet represents the four elements of the universe: fire, water, air, and earth. Fire is represented as Satan; water is Leviathan; air is Lucifer; and Earth is Belial.[31] Don't miss the fact that the Bible uses the names Satan, Leviathan, Lucifer, and Belial to refer to the devil.

If you or your forefathers were high-level Masons, you most likely will have to deal with this spirit in you. This spirit may be hidden with no manifestations occurring. But if the spirit is there, it may be waiting to rise up to destroy you just at the time you are stepping into your destiny. Don't wait until it is too late to deal with this spirit. It is important to understand what this spirit is and how it manifests in order to identify it and take it down through the power of the Holy Spirit. It can also be identified as the spirit of "Pan" or the "He-Goat."

Have you ever been to a "Toga Party"? The origin of these parties may surprise you. This was a reenactment of the nymph and he-goat orgies of the Dionysian or Bacchic Mysteries. Sexual perversion is at the root of the theme of these parties. Your participation at one of these parties may have been innocent, but you may have been spiritually "slimed" just by being there.

Baphomet seeks to seduce the bride of Christ into a union of false intimacy. It will steal the true intimacy between the bride and the Bridegroom both in the marriage relationship as well as our relationship with Christ. It is a spirit that will try to bring division into a marriage relationship, a business, a church, or even a nation. It is a spirit of perversion with a purpose to divide. It may behave like a man-hater or woman-hater. It very often is not even sexual. Again, its purpose is to divide and destroy. It came in to Sodom and Gomorrah in Genesis 19, and it also came in to Gibeah in Judges 19 just prior to the destruction of both.

The following is a list of Egyptian gods and goddesses. You may have to be delivered from one or all of these false gods/demons if you or your ancestors have participated in

Freemasonry: Aker, Amon, Anubus, Apis, Aton, Atum, Bes, Edjo, Geb, Hathor, Heket, Horus, Isis, Khepri, Khnum, Khons, Maat, Meskhenet, Min, Mut, Nekhbet, Nut, Osiris, Ptah, Ra, Sekhmet, Selket, Seshat, Seth, Shu Sobek, Sothis, Thermuthis, Thoth, and Thoueris.[32]

The following symbols/animals are also of concern: Ankh, Scepter of Seth, Scarab, Cobra, Falcon, Eye of Horus, Third Eye, All-Seeing Eye, Cats of the Egyptian Pyramids, obelisks, and all clothing and regalia associated with rituals including the apron, cabletow, blindfold, etc. This certainly is not a complete list, but it is good to be aware of them.

The following is a list of curses related to Freemasonry:

• Poverty, lack, holes in checking account or pockets
• Barrenness, miscarriages
• Breakdown of family relationship including divorce
• Pestilence—devouring of intended harvest
• Chronic sickness—chronic fatigue, allergies, blood disorders, throat and respiratory disorders, heart disorders, intestinal disorders
• Defeat and failure—your potential is never developed
• Mental illness, torment and confusion, double-mindedness, schizophrenia, insanity, autism, and learning difficulties
• Perpetual trauma—constantly putting out fires
• Accident prone
• Emotional hardness—especially in men relating with their children
• Religious spirit or controlling spirit
• Spiritual hindrances and apathy—spiritual blindness
• Premature and violent death—also death of the firstborn
• Doubt, skepticism, unbelief, and mockery—intellectualism
• Pride and arrogance
• Fear and anxiety
• Lust and sexual perversion[33]

Are you battling some of these curses? Do you want this structure in your business? We must begin by tearing down the structures of the pyramid in our personal lives and organizations. If we continue to accept the current structure with a king on top, our mindsets are prepared for the Antichrist to reign as king. If we don't establish a new organizational structure that is godly, we may find ourselves still entangled in Babylon and unable to free ourselves!

CHAPTER 6

God's Redemptive Plan
for Business Leadership

The Lord spoke through the prophet Jeremiah in Jeremiah 23:5-6.

"Behold, the days are coming," says the Lord, "That I will raise to David a Branch of righteousness; a King shall reign and prosper, and execute judgment and righteousness in the earth. In His days Judah will be saved, and Israel will dwell safely; now this is His name by which He will be called: THE LORD OUR RIGHTEOUSNESS."

Fallen mankind desires a king. He will gladly accept one of his own who will take a throne and use it for self-exaltation and to enslave those around him. However, this was not God's original plan. He gave man and woman dominion over the earth, but He intended them to rule under God's direction. This would have worked well as long as they were in constant fellowship with God. After sin entered and mankind desired to be like God, the companionship ended. However, mankind's desire to be like God did not.

In order to be like the other nations, the people of Israel cried out for a king. God knew that this was a setup for His people. There was a weakness in man to seek out divine kingship. This divine nature is part of who we are and who God made us to be, for we were made in His image.

Then God said, "Let Us make man in Our image, according to Our likeness" (Genesis 1:26).

This is the weakness that Adam and Eve had in the garden of Eden where there was no sin. They wanted to be like God, knowing good and evil. Think about it. They had everything. This was the one area in which Satan could tempt them. "It was on this point that the devil came to tempt him. He dangled before him as a possible possession the one thing a creature could never have— divinity."[1] If Adam and Eve could not overcome this in the garden, how can those following them in a fallen world overcome it?

*Then the serpent said to the woman, "You will not surely die. For God knows that in the day you eat of it your eyes will be opened, and **you will be like God**, knowing good and evil"* (Genesis 3:4-5, emphasis added).

How did Satan know of this weakness? It is the same sin that got him thrown out of heaven.

*How you are fallen from heaven, O Lucifer, son of the morning! How you are cut down to the ground, you who weakened the nations! For you have said in your heart; "I will ascend into heaven, **I will exalt my throne above the stars of God**; I will also sit on the mount of the congregation on the farthest sides of the north; I will ascend above the heights of the clouds, **I will be like the Most High**"* (Isaiah 14:12-14, emphasis added).

God's pathway to redemption and restoring mankind back to Him did include a king: King Jesus! Jesus came as a man, but He showed us how to pass the kingship test.

Again, the devil took Him up on an exceedingly high mountain, and showed Him all the kingdoms of the world and their glory. And he said to Him, "All these things I will give You if You will fall down and worship me." Then Jesus said to him, "Away with you, Satan! For it is written, you shall worship the Lord your God, and Him only you shall serve" (Matthew 4:8-10).

Jesus, in His state of humanness, chose to fast for forty days and forty nights. It was in this place of human weakness that the enemy came to tempt Him. "In each step of the temptation presented to Him, He said the resounding yes to His Father and no to Satan."[2]

Jesus had the right and authority to be God, yet He chose His position of humanness to fulfill the test that Adam could not pass. It was after passing this test that His ministry began, and He began to operate in signs and wonders. He fully understood that His ministry was not about self-exaltation but about the Father's will. As soon as we step into self-exaltation, we struggle with building the Tower of Babel. This self-exaltation is the reason why the organizational structure of the pyramid is so dangerous.

Jesus fulfilled the kingship that the people had been seeking. Jesus fulfilled the prophesy of Jeremiah 23. He was of the line of David and fulfilled the Davidic covenant.

When your days are fulfilled and you rest with your fathers, I will set up your seed after you, who will come from your body, and I will establish his kingdom. He shall build a house for My name, and I will establish the throne of his kingdom forever. I will be his Father, and he shall be My son. If he commits iniquity, I will chasten him with the rod of men and with the blows of the sons of men. But My mercy shall not depart from him, as I took it from Saul, whom I removed from before you. And your house and your kingdom shall be established forever before you. Your throne shall be established forever (2 Samuel 7:12-16).

This prophesy was twofold. The first part was fulfilled with the reign of Solomon. The second part was fulfilled with the coming of Jesus Christ. Christ's kingdom fulfilled the establishment of David's throne and kingdom being established forever.

> *And behold, you will conceive in your womb and bring forth a Son, and shall call His name Jesus. He will be great, and will be called the Son of the Highest; and the Lord God will give Him the throne of His father David. And He will reign over the house of Jacob forever, and of His kingdom there will be no end* (Luke 1:31-33).

When the captives were released from Babylon, Zerubbabel became governor of Judah. God once again established a government for the people. God did not make him a king but a governor who possessed great authority. Zerubbabel was of the line of David and also of the genealogy of Jesus.

> *The book of the genealogy of Jesus Christ, the Son of David, the son of Abraham: Abraham begot Isaac* (Matthew 1:1-2).

> *David the king begot Solomon by her who had been the wife of Uriah* (Matthew 1:6).

> *Josiah begot Jeconiah and his brothers about the time they were carried away to Babylon. And after they were brought to Babylon, Jeconiah begot Shealtiel, and Shealtiel begot Zerubbabel* (Matthew 1:11-12).

> *And Jacob begot Joseph the husband of Mary, of whom was born Jesus who is called Christ. So all the generations from Abraham to David are fourteen generations, from David until the captivity in Babylon are fourteen generations, and from the captivity in Babylon until the Christ are fourteen generations* (Matthew 1:16-17).

"The genealogy is broken down into three groups of names with fourteen generations in each list. The name David in Hebrew has a numerical value of fourteen. Because the heading of the list is 'Son of David,' Matthew may have been drawing attention to the Davidic emphasis in these names. In the first group, the Davidic throne is established; in the second group, the throne is cast down and deported to Babylon; in the third group, the throne is confirmed in the coming of the Messiah. Further, a basic covenant is set forth in each of these three periods: the Abrahamic covenant *(Genesis 12:2-3)* in the first, the Davidic covenant *(2 Samuel 7:12-16)* in the second and the New Covenant *(Hebrews 8:7-13)* in the third"[3] (emphasis added).

Zerubbabel had a covenant right to the throne, yet God made him a governor. Through Haggai, God spoke to Zerubbabel,

> *I will shake heaven and earth. I will overthrow the throne of kingdoms; I will destroy the strength of the Gentile kingdoms. I will overthrow the chariots and those who ride in them; the horses and their riders shall come down, everyone by the sword of his brother. In that day, says the Lord of hosts, I will take you Zerubbabel My servant, the son of Shealtiel, says the Lord, and will make you like a signet ring; for I have chosen you, says the Lord of Hosts* (Haggai 2:21-22).

Clearly, God had chosen Zerubbabel as His leader. This is a prophetic picture of the authority that was soon to be established through Christ in us. As God gave Zerubbabel His signet ring, He gave Zerubbabel kingly authority yet the title and position of governor. That didn't minimize who Zerubbabel was, but it protected him and prepared the heart of his people to receive their true King.

God has not called us to be kings on this earth but rulers who govern to establish the kingdom of God upon the earth. Much confusion on this topic may have come from the translation of the following Scripture:

*Now when He had taken the scroll, the four living creatures and the twenty-four elders fell down before the Lamb, each having a harp, and golden bowls full of incense, which are the prayers of the saints. And they sang a new song, saying: You are worthy to take the scroll, and to open its seals, for You were slain, and have redeemed us to God by Your blood out of every tribe and tongue and people and nation, and have made us **kings** and priests to our God; and we shall reign on the earth* (Revelation 5:8-10, emphasis added).

In the version I quote in this book, the New King James Version, the word *kings* in verse 10 of the previous passage has an asterisk mark (*) and indicates NU-Text, which reads "a kingdom."[4]

In addition, the reference Scripture is Exodus 19:6, which reads, "And you shall be to Me a kingdom of priests and a holy nation." The word *kingdom* here means, "an estate or country."[5] Therefore, we are to be an estate or country of priests unto Him. We are called to be a kingdom of priests to reign on the earth. This is very different from being kings over men.

In 1 Peter 2:9, the Word says, "But you are a chosen generation, a royal priesthood, a holy nation." In this Scripture, *royal* is a Greek word, which means just that: "royal."[6] *Webster* defines royal as, "kingly ancestry, of relating to or subject to the crown, being in the service to the crown."[7] Therefore, we are a priesthood of kingly ancestry or priesthood in service to the King. We are not called to be priestly kings.

Psalm 2 also speaks of the coming conflict between the kings of the earth and the Lord's Anointed. Let's look at Psalm 2:1-6,

*Why do the nations rage, and the people plot a vain thing? The kings of the earth set themselves, and the rulers take counsel together, against the Lord and against His **Anointed**, saying: "Let us break Their bonds in pieces and cast away Their cords from us." He who sits in the heavens shall laugh; the Lord shall hold them in derision. Then He shall speak to them in His wrath, and distress them in His deep* *displeasure:* *"Yet I have set My King on My holy hill of Zion"* (emphasis added).

Note the capital "A" on the word *Anointed* in the verse above (NKJV). The word *anointed* means, "to rub with oil, usually a consecrated person, specifically the Messiah."[8] It is capitalized in this version of Scripture because it includes Jesus and the anointed saints to battle together.

Revelation 17 states the coming battle will be against Babylon. The kings of the earth are destined to come under the authority of Babylon.

> *Then he said to me, "The waters which you saw, where the harlot sits, are peoples, multitudes, nations, and tongues. And the ten horns which you saw on the beast, these will hate the harlot, make her desolate and naked, eat her flesh and burn her with fire. For God has put it into their hearts to fulfill His purpose, to be of one mind, and to give their kingdom to the beast, until the words of God are fulfilled.* ***And the woman whom you saw is that great city which reigns over the kings of the earth"*** *(Revelation 17:15-18, emphasis added).*

If we are coming from the same structure of kingship, we will not be able to stand against Babylon. In fact, we may even find ourselves on the same side.

> *The ten horns which you saw are ten kings who have received no kingdom as yet, but they receive authority for one hour as kings with the beast. These are of one mind, and they will give their power and authority to the beast. These will make war with the Lamb, and the Lamb will overcome them, for He is* ***Lord of lords, King of kings;*** *and those who are with Him are called, chosen, and faithful* (Revelation 17:12-14, emphasis added).

We find other places in Scripture where God is declared as the God of gods, Lord of lords, and King of kings (Deuteronomy

10:17; Daniel 2:47). Just as God has not called us to be gods, He has not called us to be lords or kings. In fact, both First Peter and Mark warn against being lords over the flock entrusted to you.

*Shepherd the flock of God which is among you, serving as overseers, not by compulsion but willingly, not for dishonest gain but eagerly, nor as being **lords** over those entrusted to you, but being examples to the flock and when the Chief Shepherd appears, you will receive the crown of glory that does not fade away* (1 Peter 5:2-4, emphasis added).

*But Jesus called them to Himself and said to them, "You know that those who are considered rulers over the Gentiles **lord** it over them, and their great ones exercise authority over them. Yet is shall not be so among you; but whoever desires to become great among you shall be your servant. And whoever of you desires to be first shall be slave of all. For even the Son of Man did not come to be served, but to serve, and to give His life a ransom for many"* (Mark 10:42-44, emphasis added).

Babylon's structure is man's kingdom trying to reach heaven through the Tower of Babel or the pyramids. God's structure is the kingdom of heaven coming down to earth. Let's look at what God's court looks like.

Immediately I was in the Spirit; and behold, a throne set in heaven, and One sat on the throne. And He who sat there was like a jasper and a sardius stone in appearance; and there was a rainbow around the throne, in appearance like an emerald. Around the throne were twenty-four thrones, and on the thrones I saw twenty-four elders sitting, clothed in white robes; and they had gold crowns on their heads. And from the throne proceeded lightning, thunderings, and voices. Seven lamps of fire were burning before the throne, which are the seven Spirits of God (Revelation 4:2-5).

God sits on His throne in the center of 24 thrones that circle around His throne. The word *elder* means, "celestial council or judge."[9]

God initially intended to bring this governmental structure of heaven to earth when He established the judges of Israel. In Judges, God established judges to be political leaders who delivered Israel from foreign threat or oppression as well as settled disputes among the people.

Nevertheless the Lord raised up judges who delivered them out of the hand of those who plundered them. Yet they would not listen to their judges, but they played the harlot with other gods, and bowed down to them. They turned quickly from the way in which their fathers walked, in obeying the commandments of the Lord, they did not do so. And when the Lord raised up judges for them the Lord was with the judge and delivered them out of the hand of their enemies all the days of the judge; for the Lord was moved to pity by their groaning because of those who oppressed them and harassed them (Judges 2:16-18).

In Daniel, we see another vision of the throne room of heaven.

I watched till thrones were put in place, and the Ancient of days was seated; His garment was white as snow, and the hair of His head was like pure wool. His throne was a fiery flame, its wheels a burning fire; a fiery stream issued and came forth from before Him. A thousand thousands ministered to Him; ten thousand times ten thousand stood before Him. The court was seated and the books were opened (Daniel 7:9).

And behold, One like the Son of Man, coming with the clouds of heaven! He came to the Ancient of Days, and they brought Him near before Him. Then to Him was given dominion and glory and a kingdom, that all peoples, nations, and languages should serve Him. His dominion is an everlasting dominion, which shall not pass away, and His kingdom the one which shall not be destroyed (Daniel 7:13-14).

A kingdom will be given to the Son of Man, Jesus, that all peoples, nations, and languages will serve Him. Halleluiah! This kingdom is eternal. Praise God!

But the court [judges or elders] shall be seated, and they shall take away his dominion, to consume and destroy it forever. Then the kingdom and dominion, and the greatness of the kingdoms under the whole heaven, shall be given to the people, the saints of the Most High. [We shall receive all kingdoms into His kingdom.] ***His kingdom is an everlasting kingdom, and all dominions shall serve and obey Him*** (Daniel 7:26, emphasis added).

"The kingdom of God, governed by His saints, will exercise rule over all the earth."[10] As Zerubbabel ruled as governor with the signet ring of God, we will rule and reign over the earth. In order to reign with Christ in purity and holiness, we must begin to replace the current Babylonian structures of ourselves as kings of our own kingdoms. This means we must make God King and establish His kingdom on earth. In the next chapter, I will show you God's vision of what the new structures should look like. It is time to come out of the structure of the pyramid and get past the curses and bondages. It is time to reinvent the wheel and apply it to a new business structure so that we can step into the blessings and fullness of what we have been called to do.

CHAPTER 7

Establishing the Kingdom of Heaven in Your Business

God has given us the authority to rule and reign on the earth. So I began to ask God why my husband and I weren't seeing prosperity in our business. "Lord, I don't understand. We have dedicated our business to You and followed Your strategy. We have prayed to see the miracles like those the apostles walked in from the book of Acts, but we are not seeing it. Lord, how have we missed it?"

He gave me a vision of a pyramid and then said, "You have built man's kingdoms in your businesses, churches, and governments in the shape and structure of the Tower of Babel and the Egyptian pyramids. I am God. I am the King. It is My kingdom that is to be built. Bring My kingdom to the earth."

Then He gave me a vision of a wheel and said, "This is the wheel of Ezekiel. It is the structure of My government in heaven." I then saw God on a throne in the center with the twenty-four elders sitting all around Him. In the midst of the throne and around the throne were the four living creatures. In the midst of the living creatures and the elders stood a Lamb with seven horns and seven eyes, which are the seven spirits of God. This is the same picture from Revelation 5:6-7.

I have been so excited to share this vision with others, only to find out that they too have seen visions of wheels. God always communicates to many in the body when He is bringing new revelation.

We have learned to pray: "Our Father in heaven, hallowed be Your name. Your kingdom come. Your will be done on earth as it is in heaven." Jesus taught us to pray in this manner. We are praying for the kingdom of heaven to come into the earth, our lives, our churches, and our businesses.

Currently there are several teachings on the types of anointings in the marketplace. One is the anointings of kings and priests, where the kings make the money and support the priests. Another is the apostles/kings and prophets anointing like Cyrus and Daniel. And then there is the Joseph anointing with the storehouse principle. These are all good teachings, but God is bringing forth even greater understanding to prepare us to walk in the miracles like those that were seen by the first century church.

God showed me the structure of the pyramid as the basic organizational structure of most governments, businesses, churches, and other organizations. That structure sets individuals up to become kings over their own kingdoms. It is a structure of power, control, elitism, domination, and idolatry. Climbing the corporate ladder is all about getting to the top. Where is God in all of this?

My next question was, "Lord, how can the wheels of Ezekiel bring redemption to the marketplace?" Then I saw wheels and wheels inside of wheels. I saw wheels spinning and connected to more wheels. Then God took me to the book of Ezekiel.

*Now it came to pass in the thirtieth year, in the fourth month, on the fifth day of the month, as I was among the captives by the River Chebar, that the heavens were opened and **I saw visions of God*** (Ezekiel 1:1, emphasis added).

*Now as I looked at the living creatures, behold, a **wheel** was on the earth beside each living creature with its four faces. The appearance of the **wheels** and their workings was like the color of beryl, and all four* *had the same likeness. The appearance of their workings was, as it were, a wheel in the middle of a wheel* (Ezekiel 1:15-16, emphasis added).

*As for their rims, they were so high they were awesome; and their rims were **full of eyes**, all around the four of them* (Ezekiel 1:18, emphasis added).

*Wherever the spirit wanted to go, they went, because there the spirit went; and the wheels were lifted together with them, **for the spirit of the living creatures was in the wheels*** (Ezekiel 1:20, emphasis added).

*Like the appearance of a rainbow in a cloud on a rainy day, so was the appearance of the brightness all around it. This was the appearance of the **likeness of the glory of the Lord*** (Ezekiel 1:28, emphasis added).

The Hebrew definition of wheel in this verse is that of a chariot wheel with spokes all around. The Hebrew definition for the living creatures is the word *chay*, which means "life or substance."[1] **The spirit of the life and substance of God was in the wheels**. God was saying that even the structure of our organizations, if godly, can bring life to the organization.

God brought a very similar vision to John in Revelation.

*Immediately I was in the Spirit; and behold, a throne set in heaven, and One sat on the throne. And He who sat there was like a jasper and a sardius stone in appearance, and there was a rainbow around the throne, in appearance like an emerald. **Around the throne were twenty-four thrones, and on the thrones I saw twenty-four elders sitting, clothed in white robes; and they had crowns of gold on their heads.** And from the throne proceeded lightnings, thunderings, and voices. **Seven lamps of fire** were burning before the throne, which are* the **seven Spirits of God**. *Before the throne there was a sea of glass like crystal. And in the midst of the throne, and around the throne, were four living creatures **full of eyes** in front and in back* (Revelation 4:2-6, emphasis added).

*And I looked, and behold, in the midst of the throne and of the four living creatures and in the midst of the elders, stood a **Lamb** as though it had been slain, having **seven horns and seven eyes**, which are the **seven Spirits of God** sent out into all the earth* (Revelation 5:6, emphasis added).

Many things are being addressed in this vision. It is a picture of God's heavenly order. It is a picture of God's government. God is on the center throne with the twenty-four elders sitting around Him. In the midst of the throne and around the throne were the four living creatures. In the midst of the throne, the living creatures, and the elders stood a Lamb (Jesus) having seven horns and seven eyes, which are the seven spirits of God.

This is the picture of the wheel with spokes going outward. The center hub in heaven is God with Jesus. However, the apostle/prophet is the center hub while we are still on earth. God confirms this same structure in Ephesians.

*Now, therefore, you are no longer strangers and foreigners, but fellow citizens with the saints and members of the household of God, having been built on the **foundation** of the **apostles and prophets**, Jesus Christ Himself being the chief **cornerstone**, in whom the whole building, being fitted together, grows into a holy temple in the Lord, **in whom you also are being built together for a dwelling place of God in the Spirit*** (Ephesians 2:19-22, emphasis added).

This is the establishment of a structure that is a dwelling place or tabernacle for the glory of God. The Word tells us that we are built together on the foundation of the apostles and prophets with

Jesus being our Chief Cornerstone. This is opposed to the Masonic tradition, which states that each individual is the cornerstone with Masonry being the foundation. A cornerstone is the most basic element of the foundation. *Webster* defines *foundation* as, "the basis upon which something stands or is supported."[2] The core of the wheels is supported by the apostolic and prophetic, while we are still on earth, with Jesus being the common bond to hold it all together.

First Corinthians tells us, "when that which is perfect has come, then that which is in part will be done away." Once we "have come to the unity of the faith and of the knowledge of the Son of God," we will enter into the heavenly court with God's heavenly government.

Isaiah 11:2 gives us the seven spirits of God: "The Spirit of the Lord shall rest upon Him, the Spirit of wisdom and understanding, the Spirit of counsel and might, the Spirit of knowledge and the fear of the Lord." The Lamb, Jesus, as though it had been slain had seven horns and seven eyes, which represents the seven Spirits of God. The seven horns represent apostolic authority, and the seven eyes represent prophetic vision. Therefore, when the apostolic authority and the prophetic vision are in full operation, the seven spirits of God will manifest. It is because Jesus was the Lamb that was slain and went to be with the Father that we can walk in the fullness of His power.

Many years ago, my husband and I were praying about how we fit into the ministry we serve. God showed me a picture of a wheel made out of Tinker Toys. More recently, as I was asking for more revelation about godly business structure, God showed me the same picture—the wheels. However, it was multi-dimensional, and there were wheels within the wheels. The center position made up of the apostolic and prophetic had seven spokes that went out of it, representing the seven spirits of God. Each spoke represented a position at the end of it. That position at the end also represented an opportunity to form a wheel. As this vision grew, it was massive with wheels inside of wheels. The apostolic and prophetic were the foundations—not at the top but in the middle.

The connection of the spokes from one position to the next provided clear order, covering, financial flow, authority, and alignment. This picture of leadership showed empowerment being released outward to lift up the entire wheel or organization and not raising up an individual to the top for self-exaltation or a position of power. It was a structure established to give God, not man, the glory as King. Each position was intertwined and interdependent. There was order but not elitism.

Over and over, the Holy Spirit has taken me back to Ezekiel to study the wheels. In Ezekiel 1, he was next to the River Chebar and is given the vision of the wheels. God was trying to make a point about the wheels of Ezekiel. Then I turned to Ezekiel 8 where the Spirit shows Ezekiel the abominations in the temple. (I addressed this in a previous chapter.) This is where Masonic rituals were being practiced in the temple.

In Ezekiel 10, the glory of God departs from the temple. What is so fascinating about the glory departing is that it departs with the wheels!

> *And I looked, and there in the firmament that was above the head of the cherubim, there appeared something like a sapphire stone, having the appearance of the likeness of a throne. Then He spoke to the man clothed with linen, and said, "Go in among the **wheels**, under the cherub, fill your hands with coals of fire from among the cherubim, and scatter them over the city." And he went in as I watched* (Ezekiel 10:1-2, emphasis added).

> *As for their appearance, all four looked alike-as it were, a wheel in the middle of a wheel. When they went, they went toward any of their four directions; they did not turn aside when they went, but followed in the direction the head was facing* (Ezekiel 10:10-11).

*And their whole body, with their back, their hands, their wings and the wheels that the four had, were full of eyes all around. As for the wheels, they were called in my hearing, "Wheel" (*Ezekiel 10:12-13).

*And the cherubim were lifted up. This was the living creature I saw by the River Chebar. When the cherubim went, the **wheels** went beside them; and when the cherubim lifted their wings to mount up from the earth, the same wheels also did not turn from beside them. When the cherubim stood still, the wheels stood still, and when one was lifted up, the other lifted itself up. For the spirit of the living creature was in them. **Then the glory of the Lord departed from the threshold of the temple and stood over the cherubim** (*Ezekiel 10:15-18, emphasis added).

*And the cherubim lifted their wings and mounted up from the earth in my sight. **When they went out, the wheels were beside them;** and they stood at the door of the east gate of the Lord's house, and the **glory of the God of Israel** was above them (*Ezekiel 10:19, emphasis added).

It is very important to understand the significance of the glory of God leaving the temple because of the Masonic rituals being practiced there. The glory left with the life-giving wheels. In verse 19, the word *beside* is the Hebrew word *ummah*, which means "near, beside, and along with."[3] The living creature within the wheels is the spirit of life and substance of God. If God is established over our businesses and organizations, and that life is flowing outward with order, covering, and proper alignment in place, the fullness of God's glory can flow.

*Arise, shine; for your light has come! And the glory of the Lord is risen upon you. For behold, the darkness shall cover the earth, and deep darkness the people; but the Lord will arise over you, and His glory will be seen upon you. The Gentiles shall come to your light, and kings to the brightness of your rising (*Isaiah 60:1-3).

As you look at the following page, you will see a traditional organizational chart being transformed or reinvented into the structure of the wheels. The center wheel represents the foundation of the apostle and prophet in the very center with the first level of leadership. The hubs of the first wheel are aligned with the core but are also establishing new wheels of their own. As the wheels grow, it is very difficult to see who sits on top. In this structure, God can be given the glory as the King. There must still be order and alignment, which flows from the center out as God's governmental offices are established to equip the saints. These governmental offices are referred to as the fivefold ministry in Ephesians 4:11-16. I will show you how to apply the fivefold ministry to this new structure in the next chapter.

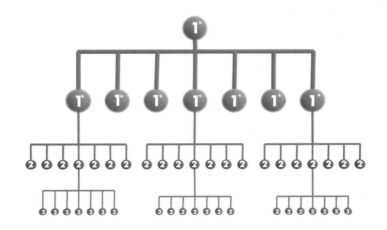

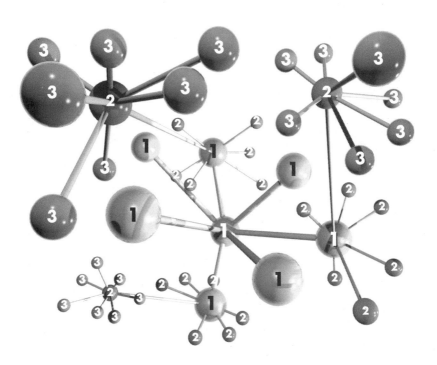

CHAPTER 8

The Power Source
of the Wheel

Our businesses need to go through a process of transfiguration so that God's light can shine in us as well as in our businesses to draw others, including nonbelievers, into His presence.

The word *transfiguration* means "a marked change in form or appearance or a metamorphosis, which brings glory and exalts." Our purpose in bringing forth transfiguration in the marketplace would result in a metamorphosis in business structure that would exalt God and bring His glory into our businesses.

The typical organizational chart presents a hierarchy in which everyone's position and purpose is to serve the vision of the one on top. As the chart, or pyramid, goes higher to the top, there is less and less room for growth and advancement. In addition, many individuals who find themselves on the bottom of the chart feel stuck, even like slaves to those who control from above. Changing the structure from a pyramid to a wheel starts the process of transfiguration; however, a heart change needs to occur as well. It is the heart and love for individuals within the organization that will bring the power source to the wheels.

I asked the Lord, "What does this look like and how does this work?" Then God gave me another picture. It was like fire superimposed upon the wheels. Again, the Lord took me to Ezekiel 10:6, "Then it happened, when He commanded the man clothed in linen, saying, 'Take fire from among the wheels, from among the cherubim.'" Then God impressed upon me that the fivefold ministry of apostles, prophets, evangelists, pastors, and teachers from Ephesians 4 was required to bring the power source or "fire" to the wheels. God showed me that the fivefold ministry is not a separate foundation and structure but more of a spiritual assignment or personality/gifting overlaid upon the wheels to bring unity, revelation, power, and redemptive purpose to the organization. It is an anointing.

Let's look again at each verse in Ephesians 4 that applies to our topic:

• Verses 11-12: "And He Himself gave some to be apostles, some prophets, some evangelists, and some pastors and teachers for the equipping of the saints for the work of ministry, for the edifying of the body of Christ." This represents spiritual offices and anointings. They are not just for the church but a lifestyle and foundation for all organizations. They bring the life substance of God into the organization. The purpose of establishing the spiritual offices is to equip the saints and edify the body of Christ. This is about building up, teaching, delivering, healing, prophesying, and restoring the body of Christ to its redemptive purpose to fulfill each individual calling as well as the calling of the organization. If the individuals as well as the leadership of an organization are in submission to the will of God, the vision of the individuals as well as the vision of the leadership will all line up to the perfect will of God. This concept is about the interaction between the center point (hub) of the wheel and each outward point at the end of a spoke.

• Verse 13: "Till we all come to the unity of the faith and of the knowledge of the Son of God, to a perfect man, to the measure of the stature of the fullness of Christ." This is about reaching that place of empowerment in unity to walk in the fullness of what God has called us to do. This applies to all of us in the marketplace too. This is also about preparing the bride for the return of Christ. Just think about how many people you can reach through the market-place that would never come into your church.

• Verse 14: "That we should no longer be children, tossed to and fro and carried about with every wind of doctrine, by the trickery of men, in the cunning craftiness of deceitful plotting." This is about exposing the lies in the worldly business structure, such as the business practices of Nimrod, the king of Tyre, and the Freemasons. We need to understand what structure is pleasing to God so we can walk in the fullness of the blessings to which we've been called.

• Verse 15: "But speaking the truth in love, may grow up in all things into Him who is the head-Christ." Again, it is about bringing forth truth in love so that the organization would mature and have an understanding that the king or head of the organization is Christ, and the purpose of the organization is to build God's kingdom.

• Verse 16: "From whom the whole body, joined and knit together by what every joint supplies, according to the effective working by which every part does its share, causes growth of the body for the edifying of itself in love." This is where each hub in the organization comes into unity with the body of the organization. When each unit is whole and is in healthy relationship with other departments, the organization can function in the purposes of God. It is from this place that the redemptive purposes of God for the organization can be fulfilled.

The biblical principles we have seen churches implement with success can also work in business transfiguration. The apostolic (leader with authority) and the prophetic (inspirational visionary) anointings must be functioning together in the center of the first or core wheel. These often work together with the prophet getting the vision or revelation and the apostle getting the physical assignment and direction to implement the vision. God miraculously draws these giftings together in the leadership of businesses and organizations. These gifts complement one another in a practical yet insightful way. With the establishment of the apostle and prophet as the organization's foundation and Jesus being the bond, God will bring the fullness of each anointing required. God has already handpicked the individuals in many organizations with all five offices or anointings, and the individuals simply need to be raised up and released into their callings.

There are many examples of all five offices in Scripture. Paul was a tentmaker. In addition, he operated as an apostle as well as a prophet. John was a fisherman who became an apostle but also pastored a local church and operated as a prophet when writing the book of Revelation.

Here are some more examples from the book of Acts:

> *Now a certain woman named Lydia heard us. She was a seller of purple from the city of Thyatira, who worshiped God. The Lord opened her heart to heed the things spoken by Paul. And when she and her household were baptized, she begged us, saying, "If you have judged me to be faithful to the Lord, come to my house and stay." So she persuaded us* (Acts 16:14-15).

Lydia was a salesperson who obviously shared the truth with her household because they were baptized. This is an example of an evangelistic anointing.

> *And he [Paul] found a certain Jew named Aquila, born in Pontus, who had recently come from Italy with his wife Priscilla and he came to them. So because he was of the same trade, he stayed with them and worked; for by occupation they were tentmakers* (Acts 18:2-3).

> *Now a certain Jew named Apollos, born at Alexandria, an eloquent man and mighty in the Scriptures, came to Ephesus. This man had been instructed in the way of the Lord; and being fervent in spirit, he spoke and taught accurately the things of the Lord, though he knew only the baptism of John. So he began to speak boldly in the syna-*

gogue. When Aquila and Priscilla heard him, they took him aside and explained to him the way of God more accurately (Acts 18:24-26).

Aquila and Priscilla were tentmakers. They were also operating in the anointing of teacher to be able to share with Apollos at a more mature level.

This process of establishing the fivefold ministry in your organization can come together quite easily if you're a small business with agreement for change among all the people. But how do we begin to transform our large corporations? How do we overlay the fivefold ministry on a business or organization that is currently in a pyramid structure?

The process starts with loving and caring for the people—by shepherding them. Do you offer counseling for your struggling employees? Have you ever thought of bringing in pastoral care alongside of Human Resources? Do you provide opportunities for your employees to continue their education either within or outside of your organization? Bible studies could be established before and after work hours for those interested. Consider establishing intercessory teams to pray for God's plan for the organization. For those units that really want to go deep, bring in restoration ministries to minister deliverance and healing for those who want it. Some of these services and more are available through The Transformation Group, LLC (see Epilogue).

This process does not have to look religious. Follow God's lead in establishing programs to reach your people. Certainly, legal questions may arise, and some business environments will facilitate this structure change with greater ease. But, most importantly, what is God saying to you for your situation? God will reward obedience.

More practically, this may begin on a personal level as individuals seek to grow and mature in the sphere where God has placed them. If you are wondering how this could apply to you, refer back to Ephesians 4.

• Verses 11-12: "And He Himself gave some to be apostles, some prophets, some evangelists, and some pastors and teachers for the equipping of the saints for the work of ministry, for the edifying of the body of Christ." Do you know your spiritual giftings? Are you operating in your giftings and equipping the body of Christ, the saints, to build God's kingdom and to exercise His dominion on the earth?

If not, what is holding you back? Do you need healing? Do you need training? Do you need mentorship or direction? Ask God to show you who He has put in your life to strengthen you and equip you to move forward in His will. Ask Him to align you with those of like mind. Seek out those people for guidance and help. Many Spirit-filled churches offer classes and small groups on many of these topics. This is where new believers join the program. The fivefold ministry equips the church or organization to bring wholeness to individuals.

• Verse 13: "Till we all come to the unity of the faith and of the knowledge of the Son of God, to a perfect man, to the measure of the stature of the fullness of Christ." In order to attain this next step, we must be in the right relationship with others of like purpose. The empowerment to move forward comes with unity and relationship with others. Are you growing in closeness with your relationships with others? Are you busy equipping the saints and new believers to move forward in their growth in stature, maturity, and wisdom? This is crucial if we are to move forward at the right time, in the right place, with the right people.

• Verse 14: "That we should no longer be children, tossed to and fro and carried about with every wind of doctrine, by the trickery of men, in the cunning craftiness of deceitful plotting." Are you continuing to grow in stature and maturity so that you can discern the schemes of the enemy and not be deceived or destroyed by them? If not, what's wrong? Are you so enjoying your new relationships and partners of unity in the body that you have neglected to maintain and grow in your relationship with the Lord? Are you falling prey to the enemy's schemes? This is not time to back down or shirk your duty. Press in and continue to grow in the new phase with these new relationships in which God has placed you.

• Verse 15: "But speaking the truth in love, may grow up in all things into Him who is the head-Christ." Are you operating with healthy lines of communication? Can you speak truth in love so that those whom God has brought you into relationship with may grow in all things? If not, are you missing truth? Then press into God so that He may give you revelation and understanding. Are your words truthful yet harsh? Remember how you operated in building up and edifying the saints? Seek healing for yourself and others if necessary.

• Verse 16: "From whom the whole body, joined and knit together by what every joint supplies, according to the effective working by which every part does its share, causes growth of the body for the edifying of itself in love." Are the relationships expanding for your group? As your sphere has learned to properly relate, grow, and mature within itself, it is ready to establish the same type of relationships with other spheres or hubs within the body of Christ within the organization.

Once individuals have accomplished unity from this place, they are ready to be the center hub of another wheel. Then the structure continues to grow as needed. Relationships with various hubs or wheels may vary depending upon the needs of each project within the organization. This process begins on an individual level but all must grow and mature together for the fullness of the glory of God to bring the life substance of God into the organization. Promotion in the organization is inherent in personal growth.

I am aware of a department in a large ministry in Colorado Springs that implemented this process with incredible success. The head of their International Ministry department established prayer times to determine God's strategy for international outreach. God directed them to invest in relationships with seemingly unimportant individuals in various countries. Not surprisingly, after these relationships were developed, those individuals came into very influential positions in these nations. These established relationships allowed this ministry to influence important governmental policy decisions and legislation, which have brought a more godly government into the lives of many people throughout the world.

This same individual with the innovative management style is currently in the lead position in the ministry. I expect to see dramatic things coming out of this ministry, for his leadership style is based on the "wheels of Ezekiel." He is a godly man who has sought to follow God every step of the way and to look for God's answers through seemingly impossible and overwhelming situations. He has taught his teams to pray for miraculous answers as God gave Gideon and Joshua.

Ministries seeking change from the structure of the world may be ready for this transition before businesses. However, we are beginning to see impressive results as businesses and even public schools are open to prayer and intercession.

One example came from a pastor of a large church in Philadelphia who approached some local businesses inquiring how his church could pray for them. He met with the president of a struggling computer firm who was interested in prayer for his business. The president shared his current accounting figures and gave the pastor specific prayer strategies for his organization. The pastor asked for quantifiable measurements so they could accurately determine the value of their prayer efforts. The pastor then established a team of intercessors to meet in the parking lot of the business and pray. After six months, impressive results came forth. In every area of quantifiable measurement, the numbers had increased. They also compared their statistics to the industry, and the results were even more dramatic.

This same pastor met with a local school in a really rough area of Philadelphia. He met with the teacher who counseled the children with the most challenging family problems and the most severe learning difficulties to determine the best prayer strategies.

Again, they assembled a team to meet in the parking lot and pray for the students. The following year, this school, which in the past had always tested in the lowest percentiles of their district, moved to the highest scores on their annual assessment tests. The teacher, who the pastor worked with initially, actually lost her job because there were no more "troubled" students left for her to teach.

These are just a few examples of a minimal approach to establishing prayer and biblical structures into the world. With a more dedicated effort, we can influence a tremendous amount of change for God's purpose and His glory.

Businesses can literally be transfigured through a shift in their structure. As the focus of leadership changes to building up and encouraging their employees, who in turn build up and encourage their customers, the organization will grow. A new level of passion comes as individuals step into their calling, realizing that it is not just a job but also their ministry. Employees can advance as they are trained to create new hubs in the wheel. This structure is fluid and dynamic, not rigid and controlling.

There is also some personal choice required. In order for this concept to work effectively, members of each wheel must be willing to seek their own levels of personal holiness through deliverance, healing, spiritual growth, and maturity.

The next three chapters will begin to help you to achieve these things in your own life.

CHAPTER 9

In the World
but not of the World

God's purpose to bring the kingdom of heaven to earth does not allow for Christians to be isolated in their comfort zones. There are seasons of our walk that God has set aside for us to grow and mature in a protected environment with more mature Christians to teach us and guide us. Then, when we are ready, we are placed in relationships that empower us to move forward and reach the world. From the position of purity, accountability, maturity, wisdom, and discernment, we can be overcomers.

As New Testament Christians, God has told us to go out into all of the world, making disciples of all the nations, to the end of the age.

Go therefore and make disciples of all the nations, baptizing them in the name of the Father and of the Son and of the Holy Spirit, teaching them to observe all things that I have commanded you; and lo, I am with you always, even to the end of the age (Matthew 28:19-20).

We move to a place of bringing His truth into the world to bring eternal life. However, we are to be in the world but not of it.

When Pilate questioned Jesus in Pilate's court, Jesus responded, "My Kingdom is not of this world" (John 18:36).

We read in 1 John 4:4, "You are of God little children, and have overcome them, because He who is in you is greater than he who is in the world." Because Jesus went to be with the Father, we are therefore able to do even greater things than Jesus did. With Jesus Christ within us, we are able to take dominion and subdue the world. We have regained the authority that Adam had in the garden, but we must walk with God in relationship.

John the Baptist prepared the way for the coming of Jesus Christ.

In those days John the Baptist came preaching in the wilderness of Judea, and saying, "Repent, for the kingdom of heaven is at hand!" (Matthew 3:1-2)

Jesus brought the kingdom of heaven with Him. Because He died on the cross for us, we are capable of being set free from the bondages brought forth from this world. It is now safe for God to allow His children to interact with the world. In fact, it is time to go into the world and bring the world into salvation.

As we saw in Leviticus, God's purpose in bringing forth His laws to the Israelites was to keep them separate and set apart. He needed to establish that the pagan practices of the Canaanites influenced their behavior. This behavior was abhorrent to God. Obviously, there was wisdom in cleanliness, healthy dietary rules, and appropriate priestly behavior; but God also brought teaching on godly moral behavior. With Jesus, God brought the kingdom of heaven onto the earth. With His Spirit in us, we are capable of being in the world but not of it. We are called out of our church and our home groups. We are called to the Gentiles as the apostles were. We are capable of taking people out of Babylon, but the key is establishing God's kingdom on earth, not our own!

The structure of our organizations is important. We must come out of creating pyramids with kings perched on top. Furthermore, when we build God's kingdom through loving and encouraging those around us, He builds our business. If we want to see the kingdom of heaven on earth, however, we must first establish a personal relationship with Jesus and walk in personal holiness. **We have to be willing to deal with our "stuff" so that there is no iniquity or sin in us with which the enemy can entrap us.** We must walk in godly character at all times, especially at our places of business. Our hearts must be pure if we are to bring freedom to those who are in bondage in our spheres of influence. What does this look like? Consider the following questions:

Who are your associates? Are those individuals godly?

What do you watch on television? What movies do you watch?

What websites do you visit on the Internet?

What do you do behind closed doors or in the dark?

Do you have secrets in your life?

Are you so busy pointing the finger at someone else that you can't see your own shortcomings?

Lifestyle evangelism is probably the most powerful form of attracting or repelling potential believers. Do they see Christ in you? Do they ask you what is so different about you? Do they know you are a Christian?

Do not think that I [Jesus] came to destroy the Law of the Prophets. I did not come to destroy but to fulfill. For assuredly, I say to you, till heaven and earth pass away, one jot or one tittle will by no means pass from the law till all is fulfilled. Whoever therefore breaks one of the least of these commandments, and teaches men so, shall be called last in the kingdom of heaven. For I say to you, that unless your righteousness exceeds the righteousness of the scribes and Pharisees, you will by no means enter the kingdom of heaven (Matthew 5:17-20).

Christ came to redeem us from the areas in our lives that are not pure. He came to set us free from our generational sin and disobedience. This is certainly not a license to sin but empowerment to overcome those lies, hurts, and iniquitous behaviors that will keep us from fulfilling everything to which God has called us.

Jesus said to him, "You shall love the Lord your God with all your heart, with all your soul, and with all your mind. This is the first and great commandment. And the second is like it: You shall love your neighbor as yourself. On these two commandments hang all the Law and the Prophets" (Matthew 22:37-40).

A relationship with the Lord is where it all starts. Think about how you felt when you were first in love. When you love someone, you want to know what that person thinks and what pleases that individual. You want to be with that person all of the time. Your priorities show your love. Where is your personal relationship with Christ? It all starts here!

The gospel of Matthew, as well as the other gospels, gives us many examples of what the kingdom of heaven should look like in our own lives:

Therefore if you bring your gift to the altar, and there remember that your brother has something against you, leave your gift there before the altar, and go your way. First be reconciled to your brother, and then come and offer your gift (Matthew 5:23-24).

Forgiveness and reconciliation are important to God. When you make an offering, your heart must be pure.

You have heard that it was said to those of old, "You shall not commit adultery." But I say to you that whoever looks at a woman to lust for her has already committed adultery with her in his heart (Matthew 5:27-28).

How many lustful actions happen at your workplace? How many computers have been checked for pornography?

Let your "Yes" be "Yes," and your "No" be "No." For whatever is more than these is from the evil one (Matthew 5:37).

You must walk in truth or you will bring a curse upon yourself, your family, and your business.

But when you do a charitable deed, do not let your left hand know what your right hand is doing, that your charitable deed may be in secret; and your Father who sees in secret will Himself reward you openly (Matthew 6:3-4).

Have you noticed Masonic dedications of hospitals and schools where the Masons are taking the glory? How many times are charitable events all about man taking glory for himself and naming the building or event after himself? All glory should be going to God. Giving openly is not a sin and is often truly meant to be a blessing. It is about where your heart is. Are you giving out of a generous heart, or to elevate yourself? It is crucial to listen to God and be obedient to Him. It is not about giving for others to see but out of obedience to God. God is really serious about this. Look at what happened to Ananias and Sapphira.

But a certain man named Ananias, with Sapphira his wife, sold a possession. And he kept back part of the proceeds, his wife also being aware of it, and brought a certain part and laid it at the apostle' feet. But Peter said, "Ananias, why has Satan filled your heart to lie to the Holy Spirit and keep back part of the price of the land for yourself?" ... Then Ananias, hearing these words, fell down and breathed his last (Acts 5:1-5).

I have struggled with this Scripture over the years because it seemed as though God was very severe to bring death to the couple even when they gave such a significant amount to the church. As I have prayed about it, God revealed that it was not about the amount that they gave. It was about their obedience and heart is-sues. The Holy Spirit told them to give the whole amount. They lied and brought forth a portion of the proceeds, saying it was the whole amount. They wanted everyone to see that they gave the proceeds to the apostle. Their hearts were about people seeing what they gave, not about obedience. Time and time again I know that God has smiled upon generous giving, even public giving. However, in these cases, it was the heart behind the gift that caused God to smile!

Do not lay up for yourselves treasures on earth, where moth and rust destroy and where thieves break in and steal; but lay up for yourselves treasures in heaven, where neither moth nor rust destroys and where thieves do not break in and steal. For where your treasure is, there your heart will be also (Matthew 6:19-21).

The old saying, "You can't take it with you when you leave" is a very true statement, but it only applies to material possessions. We can take people with us. Are you having an impact on people's des-tinies? What about their eternal destiny?

No one can serve two masters; for either he will hate one and love the other, or else he will be loyal to one and despise the other. You cannot serve God and mammon (Matthew 6:24).

I have heard teachings that compare having wealth and nice things to having a spirit of mammon. That is a lie! God wants to bless us and prosper us. In ministering to deliver the spirit of mammon, I have actually worked with many more individuals strug-gling financially who had a spirit of mammon than those who were blessed financially. I once heard it put like this, "Money is kind of like air. If you have enough of it, you don't think about it. But if you are lacking, it is all that you think about." The key is whom do you trust to be your provider? Sometimes God takes us to the end of ourselves financially to help us build faith for the miraculous. If we think that we can only prosper in our own power, how will we have enough faith for the miracle of multiplication?

In the New Testament, the miraculous is expected. The loaves and fishes principle complements the storehouse principle of the Old Testament.

> *He [Jesus] said, "Bring them here to Me." Then He commanded the multitudes to sit down on the grass. And He took the five loaves and the two fish, and looking up to heaven, He blessed and broke and gave the loaves to the disciples; and the disciples gave to the multitudes. So they all ate and were filled, and they took up twelve baskets full of the fragments that remained. Now those who had eaten were about five thousand men, besides women and children* (Matthew 14:18-21).

The miracle began by someone giving the five loaves and the two fish. This concept works like priming a well pump, which involves pouring water in the well to cause the water to flow out. Consider a strong, giving program in your business or organization to prime your pump!

Look at the attitude of the wicked and lazy servant in the parable of the talents.

> *Then he who had received the one talent came and said, "Lord, I knew you to be a hard man, reaping where you have not sown, and gathering where you have not scattered seed. And I was afraid, and went and hid your talent in the ground. Look, there you have what is yours"* (Matthew 25:24-25).

The man in this story did not understand the principle of multiplication. In multiplication, you reap even in places where you have not sown. If you are called to give to the orphans and widows (Acts 6), you most likely will not reap from the same place, but God will still honor your obedience and bless you from another source.

Sometimes we expect a financial blessing, but God blesses us in another way. It might not always look like we think it is supposed to look. The key is to give where and when God tells us to give. It involves obedience and trust in the Lord. Giving releases the anointing of multiplication. Some are even called to sell all they have.

Nor was there anyone among them who lacked; for all who were possessors of lands or houses sold them, and brought the proceeds of the things that were sold, and laid them at the apostles; feet; and they distributed to each as anyone had need (Acts 4:34-35).

We know many missionaries who have sold all their possessions to serve the Lord on the mission field. What is the Lord asking you to do?

What many Christians don't understand is that their behavior may be actually bringing about curses. Many of the curses have already been established in the family line, and an individual's vulnerability to the iniquity causes it to continue not only in their life but also in the lives of their children, grandchildren, and great-grandchildren. An example may be a curse of poverty that has come down the family line through Freemasonry. If an individual is struggling with the curse of poverty and is put in a tight place financially, the individual may become vulnerable and lie. Lying also brings poverty. Now the curse has been compounded! This will make it even more difficult to break through to prosperity for not only the individual but also future generations.

The following are examples of behaviors that have brought in curses that we have dealt with in ministry:

• Buying foreclosures (property) from widows and orphans and selling for a profit.

• Deceiving insurance companies to increase profit—doctors inflating prices to increase "Usual and Customary," and reclamation businesses sending phony invoices to recoup deductibles, etc.

• Using illegal aliens to avoid paying appropriate insurance and taxes and/or taking advantage of them by paying lower wages.

• Putting permits in clients' names to avoid fees.

• Telling lies and half-truths to convince others to look at or participate in something for that business person's own personal benefit.

• Trying to change a contract to make more money.

• Day trading—is a spirit of gambling involved?

• Selling products with higher commissions versus appropriate product for the individual (the companies use higher commissions as an incentive to the sales representative to sell the products that are the most profitable).

• Investing in mutual funds where some of the money is placed in an account that goes against God's commandments (i.e. abortion or embryonic stem cell research). Know where your money is being used.

We have seen tremendous breakthroughs in both individual lives and businesses as we help people to identify those areas where the enemy has had a foothold. One individual who is a Christian counselor shared that sometimes it is difficult to release clients once their healing is complete because of the fear of losing income. She shared that she began to pray for results that are even more dramatic and healing for her patients in an even faster time period. God honored her prayer and not only brought miraculous restoration to her patients quicker, but also brought so many more patients that she couldn't have handled them at a slower pace.

Sometimes change brings fear. Seek the Lord for truth in any areas of your business that bring a sense of uneasiness or concern. When God exposes an open door of iniquity, He also brings a strategy to close the door and establish His truth. Trust God to reveal the truth and bring breakthrough and prosperity.

Establishing the kingdom of heaven on earth begins with us reestablishing the level of intimacy with God that Adam and Eve had in the garden. Because Jesus went to be with the Father and is seated at His right hand, we are seated with Christ and have the same authority as Christ does. We now have the authority to go into the world and take dominion of it. We no longer have to be physically separated from the rest of the world. In order to walk in the fullness of what we've been called to do, however, we must be spiritually separated and set apart from the world. In John 17:13-19, Jesus prays to God regarding His disciples being in the world but not of the world.

> *But now I come to You, and these things I speak in the world, that they may have My joy fulfilled in themselves. I have given them Your word; **and the world has hated them because they are not of the world, just as I am not of the world**. I do not pray that You should take them out of the world, but that **You should keep them from the evil one. They are not of the world, just as I am not of the world**. Sanctify them by Your truth. Your word is truth. As You sent Me into the world, I also have sent them into the world. And for their sakes I sanctify Myself, that they also may be sanctified by the truth* (emphasis added).*

Jesus would also pray the same prayer on our behalf. **Be in the world but not of it.**

CHAPTER 10

Getting Babylon Out of You!

So many Christians are saved, love the Lord, and are doing their best to serve Him; but for various reasons, they are still tied to Babylon and the structure of the world. Furthermore, many have not been taught about being filled with the Holy Spirit or about the gifts of the Spirit. It is through the understanding of the fullness of our relationship with Christ, what it is to be filled with His Spirit, and how to operate in a Spirit-filled life that we attain the transfiguration and oneness with the Lord that causes us to come into the fullness of our calling.

There are four levels of our walk with the Lord. Some barely get to the first level and stay there for many years. Others (like Paul) encounter a Damascus Road experience and seem to enter into a higher level of maturity rapidly. Most of us process through four levels as the disciples did.

The first level is that of being born again and discipled.

And Jesus, walking by the Sea of Galilee, saw two brothers, Simon called Peter, and Andrew his brother, casting a net into the sea; for they were fishermen. Then He said to them, "Follow Me, and I will make you fishers of men." They immediately left their nets and followed Him. Going on from there, He saw two other brothers, James the son of Zebedee, and John his brother, in the boat with Zebedee their father, mending their nets. He called them, and immediately they left the boat and their father, and followed Him (Matthew 4:18-22).

This is a prophetic example of being born again, accepting Jesus Christ, and abandoning our previous lifestyle. Obviously, it does not always involve walking away from our parents and job, but there are evident changes that we must make, such as coming out of sin and rebellion to follow the Lord.

Luke recounts this story with even more detail.

So it was, as the multitude pressed about Him to hear the word of God, that He stood by the Lake of Gennesaret, and saw two boats standing by the lake; but the fishermen had gone from them and were washing their nets. Then He got into one of the boats, which was Simon's, and asked him to put out a little from the land. And He sat down and taught the multitudes from the boat. When He had stopped speaking, He said to Simon, "Launch out into the deep and let down your nets for a catch." But Simon answered and said to Him. "Master, we have toiled all night and caught nothing; nevertheless at Your word I will let down the net." And when they had done this, they caught a great number of fish, and their net was breaking. So they signaled to their partners in the other boat to come and help them. And they came and filled both the boats, so that they began to sink. When Simon Peter saw it, he fell down at Jesus' knees, saying, "Depart from me, for I am a sinful man, O Lord!" For he and all who were with him were astonished at the catch of fish which they had taken; and so also were James and John, the sons of Zebedee, who were partners with Simon. And Jesus said to Simon, "Do not be afraid. From now on you will catch men. So when they had brought their boats to land, they forsook all and followed Him" (Luke 5:1-11).

Encountering Jesus changed the disciples' lives. They continued to be fishermen, but that occupation took on a whole new meaning. They chose to forsake all and follow Him.

The second phase of their relationship with Jesus involved discipleship, which was a time to learn and follow Him. They followed as He went from city to city teaching. Healings, signs, and wonders followed Him. In addition, He added to His group of disciples along the way. Once they had attained the change of heart and discipleship required for the next level, Jesus appointed them to be apostles. They were now leaders with authority. His authority and His power were imparted to them. The power He gave them at this point was specific: power to cast out unclean spirits (demons) and power to heal sickness and disease.

*And when He had called His twelve **disciples** to Him, He gave them power over unclean spirits, to cast them out, and to heal all kinds of sickness and all kinds of disease. Now the names of the twelve **apostles** are these* (Matthew 10:1-2, emphasis added).

The third level could not be attained until Jesus was resurrected. Once Jesus had gone to be with His Father, the power of the Holy Spirit was released into the earth. From then on, those who believed could perform even greater works than what Jesus Himself manifested on the earth.

Most assuredly, I say to you, he who believes in Me, the works that I do he will do also; and greater works than these he will do because I go to My Father (John 14:12).

The release of the Holy Spirit began to manifest among those gathered in the upper room on the day of Pentecost.

When the day of Pentecost had fully come, they were all with one accord in one place. And suddenly there came a sound from heaven, as of a rushing mighty wind, and it filled the whole house where they were sitting. Then there appeared to them divided tongues, as of fire, and one sat upon each of them. And they were all filled with the Holy

Spirit and began to speak with other tongues, as the Spirit gave them utterance (Acts 2:1-4).

The book of Acts then shares many miracles that the apostles did that were far beyond the casting out of demons and healing of the sick. Their anointing, passed onto handkerchiefs and shadows, healed the sick; and Philip was even supernaturally transported to another location. Intimacy in our relationship with Jesus Christ brings us into a greater manifestation of the miraculous and a better understanding of the fullness of the spiritual authority Jesus has given to us.

The fourth level is that of transfiguration, a marked change in form or appearance or metamorphosis that glorifies and exalts God. Attaining this level is to stand with King Jesus and rule with authority from heaven. We see this in the book of Revelation as the anointing of the two witnesses.

And I will give power to my two witnesses, and they will prophesy one thousand two hundred and sixty days, clothed in sackcloth. These are the two olive trees and the two lampstands standing before the God of the earth. And if anyone wants to harm them, fire proceeds from their mouth and devours their enemies. And if anyone wants to harm them, he must be killed in this manner. These have power to shut heaven, so that no rain falls in the days of their prophecy; and they have power over waters to turn them to blood, and to strike the earth with all plagues, as often as they desire (Revelation 11:3-6).

This anointing is made up of the combined anointings of the apostle and the prophet. It is a powerful anointing with authority and understanding to take dominion over nature. This is also a picture of the anointings in which Moses and Elijah were called to walk. In First Kings 17:1, Elijah shut the heavens and no rain fell. In Exodus 7-12, Moses spoke the plagues over Egypt. This is an end time anointing filled with the fire of God.

These anointings were ones in which Moses and Elijah were called by God to walk. Neither Moses nor Elijah completed all that God had planned for them in the Old Testament.

The word *apostle* does not appear anywhere in the Old Testament. However, the words *anointing* and *assignment* do. The following are characteristics of the apostolic anointing: to expand, to build, to clean the house, to pioneer and explore, to map the course, to be a visionary, to bring strategy for battle, to war, to fulfill and cast the vision, to be mobile, to focus on leaders and leadership, to establish the work, to tear down and root out, to lead the way through, to appoint, to go to the battlefield, to enforce God's will, and to lead to prevail.[1] As we read about the life of Moses, it is very clear that he missed it! There are, however, certain characteristics that he did fulfill, such as building the tabernacle (Exodus 37), warring when he held the rod of authority in the battle against the Amalakites (Exodus 17), tearing down and rooting out the principalities in Egypt (Exodus 7), and appointing the "heads of the people: rulers of thousands, rulers of hundreds, rulers of fifties, and rulers of tens" (Exodus 18:25). Yet his areas of weakness in not fulfilling the apostolic role kept him from leading the Israelites into their destiny. "In his rage, Moses did not speak to the rock as God had commended. Instead he raised his rod and struck the rock twice. When he disobeyed, Moses violated all that he had stood for over the last forty years! God was not displaying anger, but Moses fell into deliberate, unrighteous anger. And in his anger, Moses lost his own stake in the Promised Land. What a huge loss for just a moment of disobedience!"[2] So even though Moses led the Israelites for forty years through the wilderness, God did not allow him to enter the Promised Land.

Moses displayed other weaknesses as well. When God first approached Moses to lead the Israelites out of Egypt, Moses said, "O my Lord, I am not eloquent, neither before nor since You have spoken to Your servant; but I am slow of speech and slow of tongue" (Exodus 4:10). And then, "O my Lord, please send by the hand of whomever else You may send" (Exodus 4:13). Moses struggled with worthlessness and asked God to choose someone else. God did allow Moses to bring his brother Aaron. Moses sometimes pushed Aaron out in front of himself to deal with the issues God had called Moses to handle (Exodus 7-12). Anger, rage, worthlessness, arrogance, passivity, and false authority all come against the anointing of the apostle. Moses did not overcome these areas of weakness in his life in the Old Testament, which cost Moses his promise.

The characteristics of the prophetic anointing are as follows: to stir, to encourage, to shake the house, to inspire, to change the course, to be creative, to call for battle, to be a dreamer, to see the vision, to be functional, to focus on the throne of God, to experience the work, to challenge, to reveal the way, to anoint, to take you into relationship, to see the will of God, and to lead in travail.[3] Elijah was someone who did walk in his assignment as a prophet, and he was obedient to the Lord. However, Elijah struggled with victimization, which also cost him the fullness of his potential.

I have been very zealous for the Lord God of hosts; for the children of Israel have forsaken Your covenant, torn down Your altars, and killed Your prophets with the sword. **I alone am left; and they seek to take my life** (1 Kings 19:10 and 1 Kings 19:14, emphasis added).

God responded to Elijah by asking him to anoint two future kings and to find his replacement (Elisha). Basically, Elijah said he was done, to which God responded, "Okay, find your replacement, and I'll bring you home in a chariot." Some of the weaknesses that come against the prophetic anointing are as follows: victimization, abuse from authority, control and manipulation, witchcraft, divination, the religious spirit, and the false prophet.

Moses and Elijah were obviously both incredible men of God. God knew this and gave them another chance to be overcomers in the New Testament. You may ask, "How?" It was when they met Jesus during the transfiguration.

Now after six days Jesus took Peter, James, and John, and led them up on a high mountain apart by themselves; and He was transfigured before them. His clothes became shining, exceedingly white, like snow, such as no launderer on earth can whiten them. And Elijah appeared to them with Moses, and they were talking with Jesus (Mark 9:2-4).

Are you ready for your transfiguration? Are you willing to go through the fire? At the transfiguration, both Moses and Elijah met Jesus, and through Him they were purified and delivered. Most importantly, they were redeemed.

We are now back to the question that titles this chapter: How do I get Babylon out of me? This is a process of restoration and transfiguration. We must go deep into our generational past and deep into our own hurts and uncover all of the lies that we have believed through the years. We must be willing to be delivered, healed, and transfigured. It is a process of true freedom. This brings us to a place of walking in the fullness of covenant that has been given to us freely from Christ when we accepted Him as our Savior.

If you would like to renew your covenant with Christ or would like to step into the process of transfiguration, pray the following prayer out loud:

Father God, I humbly come before You. Lord, forgive me, for I am a sinner. Remove all of the grave clothes of the past and prepare a new destiny, Your destiny for me. I release all of my expectations, agendas, plans, goals, lusts, unclean thoughts, and everything else that has blocked my potential, in becoming all that You have called me to be. I accept You, Lord, into every area of my heart and life to be my Lord and Savior. Allow every area in me to be born anew in You. Lord, baptize me with Your love, fire, and the fullness of the Holy Spirit. I accept all that You have for me.

Lord, I ask that You will begin to show me all of the areas of sin in my life, both known and unknown. Show me all of the areas of generational iniquity that have allowed curses to come upon my family and me. Expose every root and every lie. I give You free reign of my life regardless of the pain. Lord, heal every tear and every hurt that I have carried. Transform my life so that I can be a holy vessel for Your use. I claim my deliverance, healing, restoration, and full transfiguration. In Jesus' name, amen.

Some of you may want to pray the following prayer for your business:

Father God, I lay down my business at Your feet. Lord, I give up all of my plans, expectations, agendas, goals, and everything else that has blocked the potential of my business from being all that You have called it to be. Please show me the redemptive purpose of my business. Show me what You have called it to be. Lord, I ask that You will reveal to me any areas of my business that have been built on the systems of Babylon and Freemasonry. Show me every area of my finances that are connected to the Illuminati. Show me where divine kingship may have been established, for I do not want to operate as the king of Tyre. Lord, I want to release all into Your kingdom and reign over all the earth with you. Bring me strategy, knowledge, and wisdom. In Jesus' name, amen.

CHAPTER 11

Reigning With the King

When we accept Jesus Christ, when He is in us and we are in Him, we actually sit together with Him in heaven. We reign with Him from His throne in heaven. The key is that we *must* be obedient. God will not give us that level of authority if He cannot trust us. We each go through a process of testing and are given the amount of responsibility that we can handle. Doesn't that sound like a good father?

We must be willing to go through the training process as the disciples did in our maturation process in order to come into the fullness and understanding required to reign with Him. When we are this connected to God, there is no question about our obedience. We cannot miss this. It is available to everyone. The question is, will we embrace it?

When the final level of training is attained, we step into that place of priesthood where we intercede daily before the throne as a kingdom of priests to our God. This is that final level in the transfiguration process that was presented in the previous chapter. At this level, we are able to speak into the earth and command it to come into alignment with the covenant purposes of God, and the earth must respond. This is a position of truly bringing heaven to earth and speaking with the level of authority of the two witnesses.

As we are coming up to this level, we must learn a new prayer strategy. When we understand our position in Christ to subdue and take dominion over the earth, we will see the fullness of the apostolic power of Christ. We are each given a sphere of influence.

It is our responsibility to bring godly influence into this sphere for kingdom purposes. We must go beyond petition prayers. So many of the prayers that we invoke, He has already done. We need to command the earth and the atmosphere to release those things that have already been completed in the spiritual to come into the physical. We need to call them into their time, into the now. We need to pray as God taught Job to pray.[1]

Have you commanded the morning since your days began, and caused the dawn to know its place. That it might take hold of the ends of the earth, and the wicked be shaken out of it? (Job 38:12-13).

God established the earth to bless us.

Thus says the Lord, "Who gives the sun for a light by day, the ordinances of the moon and the stars for a light by night, Who disturbs the sea, and its waves roar (the Lord of hosts is His name): If those ordinances depart from before Me, says the Lord, then the seed of Israel shall also cease from being a nation before Me forever" (Jeremiah 31:35).

Webster defines ordinances as "an authoritative decree of direction, order, a law set forth by a governmental authority."[2] God has ordained the earth to respond to us and to bless us. We must expect it to do so. We must step into our personal sphere of influence with authority and prepare for the battle for the kingdom of God.

God speaks of the four winds from the four quarters of heaven, which go out to scatter the enemy and come forth to bring restoration.

Thus says the Lord of hosts: "Behold, I will break the bow of Elam, the foremost of their might. **Against Elam I will bring the four winds from the four quarters of heaven, and scatter them toward all those winds;** *there shall be no nations where the outcasts of Elam* *will not go. For I will cause Elam to be dismayed before their enemies and before those who seek their life. I will bring disaster upon them, My fierce anger," says the Lord* (Jeremiah 49:35-37 emphasis added).

Also He said to me [Ezekiel], *"Prophesy to the breath, prophesy, son of man, and say to the breath, 'Thus says the Lord God: "Come from the four winds. O breath, and breathe on these slain, that they may live."'" So I prophesied as He commanded me, and breath came into them, and they lived, and stood upon their feet, and exceedingly great army* (Ezekiel 37:9-10, emphasis added).

We can call forth the four winds from the four corners of heaven to fulfill the will of God in our lives, our businesses, our finances, and all other areas God wants to redeem. There is power in our proclamations!

We must be prepared to lead our businesses with the Chief Cornerstone as our substructure, and the mature apostle and prophet as the core of our foundation, with the wheels of Ezekiel flowing with the life substance of God. Once we have the fivefold ministry in place with the glory of God filling the godly structure of our businesses, we will reign with Christ over every place that we have been given influence. From this position, we will see miracle after miracle after miracle. From this position, we will win more souls to Christ than ever before. From this position, we will influence not only people's lives on this earth, but also their souls and their legacy for all eternity. **Now that is what we are called to do!**

All authority has been given to Me in heaven and on earth. Go therefore and make disciples of all the nations, baptizing them in the name of the Father and of the Son and of the Holy Spirit, teaching them to observe all things that I have commanded you, and lo, I am with you always, even to the end of the age (Matthew 28:18-20).

Please join with me and pray the following prayer of commitment:

Father God, thank You for Your Son, Jesus Christ. Thank You for the opportunity to be one with You. I accept this relationship and this authority. Lord, do all that You must do in my life to prepare me to succeed in this plan to which You have called me. Teach me to walk in the fullness of the authority that You have made available to us who believe. Teach me to walk in the signs and wonders as the apostles did in the book of Acts. Prepare me to stand as the two witnesses stood and command the earth to respond to my words as they line up with Your purpose. I fully release my life unto You. Do with my life that which is pleasing to You. In Jesus' name, amen.

EPILOGUE

The wheel has been reinvented to bring a new structure to business. It replaces the pyramid, which has been the fundamental structure of organizational charts around the world since the ancient times. This shift is not just about structure but also about mindset. As we make this shift, we can watch the marketplace go through a process of transfiguration that is a metamorphosis, which brings God's glory into our businesses as never before.

As the prophetic anointing brings revelation and vision of this new move, ask the Lord to bring forth the apostolic anointing to help you bring the revelation into a plan of action for your organization. We have established a Pastoral Care Employer/Employee Assistance Program called The Transformation Group, LLC. Its purpose is to help you bring transfiguration into your organization in every aspect, from reestablishing your structural foundations to ministering God's healing to individuals. Our ultimate purpose is to equip your organization to fulfill all that God has called you to do. We have ministry teams representing the fivefold ministry available to help in all aspects of your transfiguration. If you have questions or would like assistance in any aspect of this transition, please visit us at www.transgroupllc.com, call 719-282-3068, or email us at linda@transgroupllc.com.

I hope this book has inspired you to see the redemptive purpose of your business or organization as God sees it. It is our job as end time Christians in the marketplace to prepare the way for this transformation to see God move again as He did in the book of Acts. Rise up, apostles and prophets. Join together with others of like mind to walk in the anointing of the two witnesses and together change the world for the purposes of God.

Endnotes

Introduction

[1] The Free Dictionary By Fairfax, 5/9/2008. http://www.thrfreedictionary.com/reinventing.

[2] The Free Dictionary By Fairfax, 5/9/2008. http://www.thrfreedictionary.com/transfiguration.

Chapter 1

1 Naomi Dowdy, *Strength to Stand*, (Naomi Dowdy Ministries, 2007), 54.

Chapter 2

1 David Livingston, "Ancient Days: Who Were the Sons of God in Genesis 6?" www.ancientdays.net/sonsofgod.htm (January 29, 2008).

2 Ibid.

3 James Strong, S.T.D., L.L.D., *The Exhaustive Concordance of the Bible*, (Madison, N.J.: AbingdonPress, 1890), *Hebrew and Chaldee Dictionary*, 79.

4 Bryce Self, "Nimrod, Mars and the Marduk Connection," www.ldolphin.org/Nimrod.html (April 14, 2007).

5 Thomas Nelson, Inc., *The Nelson Study Bible New King James Version* (Nashville, T.N.; Thomas Nelson Publishers, 1979), 205.

6 Strong, 47.

7 Strong, 25.

8 Self.

9 Strong, 117.

10 G. Edward Foryan, "Semiramis," *www.ldolphin.org/Nimrod.html* (October 24, 2007) Semiramis was famed for her beauty, strength, wisdom, voluptuousness, and alluring power and seduction. She had a man's strength of body and possessed more than a man's power of mind and force of will. Research also suggests that Semiramis was Nimrod's mother as well as his wife.

11 David Livingston, "Ancient Days: The Fall of the Moon City"; "Jericho" *www.ancientdays.net/mooncity.htm* (November 30, 2006).

12 These became the Babylonian fish gods (Merman-also known as Dagon and Mermaid).

13 Nelson, 1186. Nebo was the god of fate, writing, and wisdom.

14 This spirit brings a sense of false security. It also operates in witchcraft (sorcery, divination, and enchantments). It brings in the spirit of the false prophet.

15 These spirits or gods that began in the foundations of Babel or Babylon are the same spirits with different names that we find manifesting in different cultures. As the people were scattered, each different people group, or culture, brought their god with them. For example, Nimrod and Semiramis (or Marduk and Astarte) in Babylon also manifest as Osiris and Isis in Egypt (Masonic). They also manifest as Baal and Ashtoreth in the Canaanites cities. Ralph Edward Woodrow, *Babylon Mystery Religion, Ancient and Modern*, (Riverside, CA, 1966), 8.

Chapter 3

1 G&C Merriam Company, *Webster's New Collegiate Dictionary*, (Springfield, MA, 1980), 1179.

2 Strong, 56.

3 Livingston.

4 Ibid.

5 Kathleen Kenyan, *Digging Up Jericho: The Results of the Jericho Excavation*, (New York: Praeger, 1957), n.p. Research of an archeological dig of Jericho points out that there were "niche's" and "columns" which would suggest the worship of these demon gods.

6 "The Economy of Jubilee," *www.torahtimes.org/Biblical %20Chronology%20In%20Depth%20_A%20005_77_79.pdf.*

Chapter 4

1 Strong, 47.

2 The Masons establish monuments and obelisks representing a phallus.

3 Strong, 81.

4 Ibid., 85.

5 Ibid., 52.

6 Nelson, 1457.

7 Ibid., 684.

8 Yvonne Kitchen, *Freemasonry, Death in the Family*, (Mountain Gate, Victoria, Australia: Fruitful Vine Publishing House, 2002), n.p.

9 Nelson, 580.

10 Ibid., 583.

11 Ibid., 568.

12 Please note, there are two types of slavery and kingship addressed in this book. One is physical and the other is spiritual. Physical slavery is actual forced labor. Spiritual slavery is being in bondage to or being underneath something. Physical divine kingship is actually walking through the procession and allowing demon possession. Spiritual kingship is a heart issue that may open the door for the curses of divine kingship to affect both you and your family line.

13 Nelson, 1345.

14 "Ishtar, Lady of Heaven," *www.mystae.com.restrictd/streams/ Ishtar.html* (September 26, 2006).

15 "The Symbolism of Freemasonry: XXVII. The Sprig of Acacia," *www.sacred-texts.com/mas/sof/sof30.html* (September 26, 2006).

16 "Alexander Takes Tyre," Alexander the Great: the fall of Tyre, *www.livius.org/aj-al/alexander/alexander_t09.html* (May 17, 2008).

Chapter 5

1 "North American Currency Union," Wikipedia, The Free Encyclopedia, *www.en.wikipedia.org/wiki/Amero* (November 20, 2007).

2 Press Release, "Joint Statement" (March 23, 2005).

3 Jerome R. Corsi, "Bush Administration Quietly Plans NAFTA Super Highway," *wwwhumanevents.com/artucke.php?id=15497* (June 12, 2006).

4 Ibid.

5 *www.sirbacon.org/graphics/largeve.gif*

6 "Illuminati," Wikipedia, the Free Encyclopedia. *www.en.wikipedia.org.wiki/Illuminati* (February 28, 2007).

7 The Columbia Encyclopedia, Sixth Edition, *www.encyclopedia.com/topic/Illuminati.aspx* (August 20, 2008).

8 Dr. Stanley Monteith, *Brotherhood of Darkness*, (Oklahoma City, OK: Hearthstone Publishing, 2000), n.p.

9 "Illuminati," Wikipedia, the Free Encyclopedia. *www.en.wikipedia.org.wiki/Illuminati* (February 28, 2007).

10 Dr. Stanley Monteith, *Brotherhood of Darkness*, (Oklahoma City, OK: Hearthstone Publishing, 2000), pg. 32-33.

11 G. Edward Griffin, *The Creature from Jekyll Island*, (Appleton, WI, American Opinion Publishing, Inc., 1995), 325.

12 Yvonne Kitchen, *Freemasonry, Death in the Family*, (Mountain Gate, Victoria, Australia: Fruitful Vine Publishing House, 2002), 12.

13 Ibid., 46.

14 Kitchen, 213.

15 Ibid., 211-212.

16 Ibid., 13.

17 Steve Van Nattan, "Famous Freemasons," *www.cephasministry.com/famous.htmi* (November 20, 2007).

18 Kitchen, 127.

19 Kitchen, 53.

20 Ibid.

21 Ibid.

22 Ibid., 54.

23 Ibid., 54-55.

24 Ibid, 56.

25 Ibid., 58.

26 Ibid., 59-60.

27 Ibid, 63.

28 Ibid., 66.

29 Ibid., 61-66.

30 Ibid., 35-38.

31 *www.churchofsatinist*, Baphomet Gallery, (January 2008).

32 Thomas Nelson, Inc., *Nelson's Complete Book of Bible Maps & Charts*, (Thomas Nelson Publishers, 1996 & 1993.), 26.

33 Ron G. Campbell, *Free From Freemasonry*, (Ventura, CA: Regal Books, 1999), 168-171.

Chapter 6
1 Malcolm Smith, *The Power of the Blood Covenant*, (Tulsa, OK: Harrison House, 2002), 26-27.

2 Ibid., 80.

3 Nelson, 1575-1576.

4 NU-Text "These variations from the traditional text generally represent the Alexandrian or Egyptian type of text described previously

in "The New Testament Text." They are found in the critical text published in the 27th edition of the Nestle-Aland Greek New Testament (N) and in the United Bible societies fourth edition (U), hence the acronym 'NU-Text'" (November 24, 2007).

5 Strong, 67.

6 Ibid., 18.

7 G & C Merriam Company, *Webster's New Collegiate Dictionary*, (Springfield, MA, 1980), 1002.

8 Ibid., 73-74.

9 Ibid., 60.

10 Nelson, 1433.

Chapter 7

1 Strong, 38.

2 G & C Merriam Company, *Webster's New Collegiate Dictionary*, (Springfield, MA, 1980), 450.

3 Ibid., 89.

Chapter 10

1 Dowdy, 62.

2 Nelson, 263.

3 Dowdy, 62.

Chapter 11

1 Emmanuel Nuhu Kure, *The Apostolic Invasion*, (Kafanchan, Nigeria: Rehoboth Publishing, 1999), 107.

2 G & C Merriam Company, *Webster's New Collegiate Dictionary*, (Springfield, MA, 1980), 801.